Fact File 2013

Statistics brought alive!

@nd online

Complete Issues
articles • opinions • statistics • contacts

Get instant online access to this book by logging on to:
www.completeissues.co.uk

User name:_____

_____

CAREL PRESS
www.carelpress.com

L0065934

Reference plete Issues ⟶

Editor: Christine Shepherd

The numbers behind the issues and controversies

The copiable book

The book has important statistics presented in an attractive and stimulating way. Readers will want to look at the figures and engage with the issues.

We've looked at hundreds of sources to select figures which are relevant to the curriculum and to the lives of young people. The book is ideal for reference or the sheer pleasure of browsing. It is also fully copiable – for research or classroom use.

Online

We are constantly expanding our online service. We have now integrated our three major publications – Fact File, Essential Articles and Key Organisations – in the Complete Issues Website. This allows you to search and browse all the books together, past and present editions, and to view and download those you've purchased. It is your one-stop source of facts, figures, opinions and further research. Go to: www.completeissues.co.uk

You can access all the statistics in Fact File as PDFs. We also provide you with the raw data and links to the sources. This makes it easy for staff or students to take research further and to create your own graphs using our data. You even have access to the archive of previous editions, giving you a wealth of statistics to use. Just typing a search term in www.completeissues.co.uk will produce all the pages you need - along with related articles and organisations.

Your purchase of the book entitles you to use the online service on one computer, however, buying a site licence makes the service and the material available to **all** students and staff at **all** times, even from home. **The site licence is included in the Complete Issues Package.**

If you do not yet have the other publications in the Complete Issues Package you can upgrade by contacting us (details below).

Activate your online access now at www.completeissues.co.uk/admin. Your admin login codes are on the covering letter – if anything isn't clear, please get in touch.

We have included a checklist poster of major topics and key words in the current Fact File and Essential Articles for you to display. You can record your log-in details there and on the front page of this book to make access to the online service quick and easy.

Unique features

Up-to-date: A new edition is published every year using the latest statistics.

Relevant: To the UK, its education system and the concerns of young people.

Organised: Statistics are grouped by theme, cross referenced, indexed and linked on the page to closely related statistics. Our online searches will find even more!

Attractive: Full colour and eye-catching with appealingly designed pages and great photos.

Easy to use: You don't have to worry about copyright issues as we've cleared these. Because you have both the book and online access you can use Fact File in different ways with different groups and in different locations. You can simultaneously use it in the library, in the classroom and at home.

Flexible: You can make paper copies, use a whiteboard or a computer. Different groups or individuals can use different parts of the book at the same time. Having the raw data makes it even more adaptable.

Boosts library use: The posters provided free with each volume list the topics in Fact File and its sister publication Essential Articles and make it very easy to research issues. You can put one of your free posters in the library/LRC and one elsewhere – in the staff room, in a corridor, in a subject area. If you would like more copies of the poster just let us know.

Safe: Although we have included controversial topics and tackled difficult subjects, you can be confident that students are not going to encounter inappropriate material that an internet search might generate.

Accessible: Many of our statistics come from complex reports and are difficult to understand in their original form. The attractive and clear graphical presentation makes them accessible to young people – and the use of key words makes them easy to find.

Additional benefits: Subscribers to Essential Articles and Fact File are entitled to 10% discount on all our other products. They also receive occasional free posters to help promote library use and reading in general.

Published by Carel Press Ltd
4 Hewson St, Carlisle CA2 5AU
Tel +44 (0)1228 538928, Fax 591816
office@carelpress.co.uk
www.carelpress.com
© Carel Press

Research, design and editorial team:
Jack Gregory, Anne Louise Kershaw, Debbie Maxwell, Christine A Shepherd, Thomas Demol, Chas White

Cover design: Anne Louise Kershaw

Subscriptions: Ann Batey (Manager),
Brenda Hughes, Anne Maclagan

British Library Cataloguing in Publication Data
Fact File 2013 : essential statistics for today's key issues.
1. Great Britain--Statistics.
I. Shepherd, Christine A., 1951-
314.1
ISBN 978-1-905600-32-8

Printed by Finemark, Poland

FACT FILE 2013 CONTENTS

47 % of people said they miss their pet more than their family while they're away
page 26

PHOTO: FEATUREFLASH / SHUTTERSTOCK.COM

> 49% of adults think British children are beginning to behave like animals
>
> *page 82*

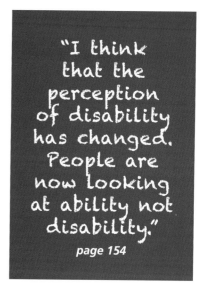

"I think that the perception of disability has changed. People are now looking at ability not disability."
page 154

More than half the young people in Spain and Greece are unemployed
page 188

Alcohol, drugs & smoking

Smoking: the facts

Smoking is the single greatest avoidable risk factor for cancer and causes nearly a fifth of all cancer cases in the UK

Smoking is the cause of **28%** of all deaths from cancer and has killed an estimated **6.5 million** people over the last 50 years.

Cigarette smoke contains a poisonous cocktail of more than 7 cancer-causing chemicals.

When a cigarette is smoked, these chemicals can enter the bloodstream and travel around the body increasing the risk of cancer in 14 areas of the body.

Tobacco causes 14 types of cancer

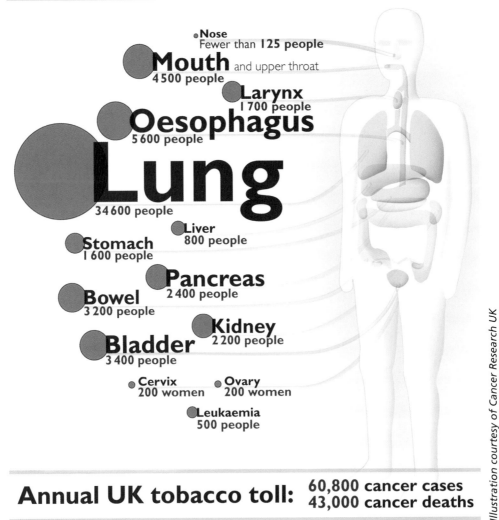

Nose
Fewer than **125 people**

Mouth and upper throat
4500 people

Larynx
1700 people

Oesophagus
5600 people

Lung
34600 people

Liver
800 people

Stomach
1600 people

Pancreas
2400 people

Bowel
3200 people

Kidney
2200 people

Bladder
3400 people

Cervix
200 women

Ovary
200 women

Leukaemia
500 people

Illustration courtesy of Cancer Research UK

Annual UK tobacco toll: 60,800 cancer cases / 43,000 cancer deaths

Together we will beat cancer

 CANCER RESEARCH UK

The average life expectancy in the UK is 78.2 for males and 82.3 for females, but a **quarter** of smokers die in middle age – between 35 and 69.

80% of smokers start smoking by the time they turn 19.

Around **20%** of the UK population smoke.

Around **half** of all long-term smokers will die from cancer or other smoking-related illnesses.

Smoking causes around **87% of lung** cancer deaths in men and around **83%** of **lung cancer deaths** in **women** in the UK.

Around **157,000** 11-15 year olds started smoking in the UK in 2010.

There is a shocking level of ignorance about smoking and cancer among the UK public.

When asked to select cancers linked to smoking, **more than 80%** of the 4,099 UK adults surveyed did not know there was a link between smoking and **eight** different cancers.

At least **two thirds** knew smoking caused cancers of the lung, mouth (oral) and throat (larynx and oesophagus), but **less than 20%** knew tobacco was linked to leukaemia and cancers of the liver, pancreas, bowel (colorectum), kidney, bladder, cervix and ovary.

Which, if any, of the following types of cancers do you think are linked to smoking?
(people were allowed to select any they thought were correct)

Lung	93%
Oral	76%
Larynx	68%
Oesophagus	66%
Stomach	38%
Liver	19%
Pancreatic	18%
Kidney	15%
Leukaemia	15%
Bladder	14%
Cervix	13%
Colorectum	13%
Ovary	12%
None of these	1%
Don't know	4%

Source: YouGov Plc survey for Cancer Research UK, 2012
www.cancerresearchuk.org/
www.yougov.co.uk

SEE ALSO:
www.completeissues.co.uk

Habit of a lifetime

64% of smokers would like to give up – but the pull of nicotine is very strong

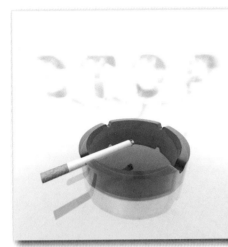

Because smoking is the leading cause of preventable illness and premature death in Great Britain there have been a number of government actions aimed to reduce it:

- In 2003 advertising on billboards and in the press was stopped.
- Smoking was banned in enclosed places in Scotland in 2006 and in England and Wales in 2007.
- In 2007 it became illegal to sell tobacco products to anyone under the age of 18.

But have these measures had any effect?

Percentage of people aged 16 and over who smoke

2003	2004	2005	2006	2007	2008	2009	2010
26	25	24	22	21	21	21	20

Proportion of smokers who...

...would find it difficult to go without smoking for a day

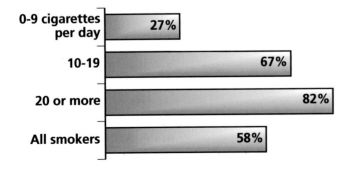

0-9 cigarettes per day	27%
10-19	67%
20 or more	82%
All smokers	58%

...have their first cigarette within five minutes of waking

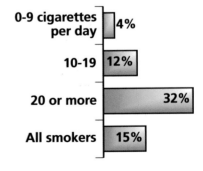

0-9 cigarettes per day	4%
10-19	12%
20 or more	32%
All smokers	15%

*All figures are GB 2010. It is likely that the survey underestimates cigarette consumption as evidence suggests that when people are asked how many cigarettes they smoke each day, there is a tendency to round the figure down to the nearest multiple of 10.

Most smokers start young

Starting young seems to lead to heavier smoking

Age at which started smoking (people aged 16 and over who had ever smoked regularly)

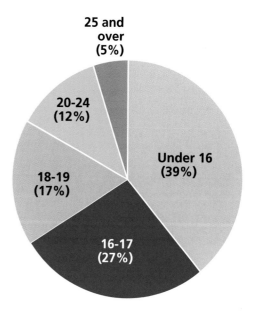

25 and over (5%)
20-24 (12%)
18-19 (17%)
Under 16 (39%)
16-17 (27%)

All current smokers, by age started

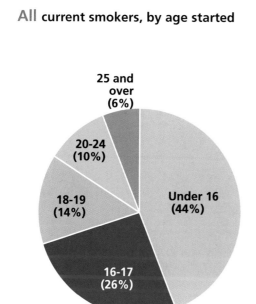

25 and over (6%)
20-24 (10%)
18-19 (14%)
Under 16 (44%)
16-17 (26%)

Current smokers who smoke twenty or more a day, by age started

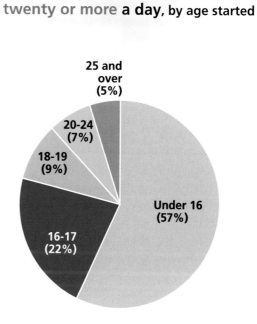

25 and over (5%)
20-24 (7%)
18-19 (9%)
Under 16 (57%)
16-17 (22%)

Source: General Lifestyle Survey Overview, ONS © crown copyright 2012
www.ons.gov.uk

SEE ALSO:
www.completeissues.co.uk

A glass too far

Some of us are drinking too much, despite the costs to health – and to the NHS

What is a unit of alcohol?

It is equivalent to half a pint of ordinary strength beer, lager or cider or a small pub measure (25ml) of spirits

Average UNITS of alcohol consumed in a week, by age, Great Britain, 2010

(Base: 42,891)

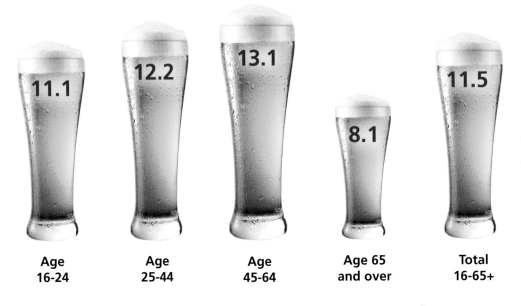

Age 16-24	Age 25-44	Age 45-64	Age 65 and over	Total 16-65+
11.1	12.2	13.1	8.1	11.5

The number of units in a drink depends on the size of the glass and the strength of the drink.

ABV (Alcohol By Volume) tells you the percentage of alcohol in the drink.

Pint of beer, lager or cider

Regular (ABV 4%)
2.3 units

Strong (ABV 5.2%)
3.0 units

Extra strong (ABV 8%)
4.5 units

Red, white or rosé wine (ABV 13%)

Small 125 ml
1.6 units

Standard 175 ml
2.3 units

Large 250 ml
3.3 units

Men
Should not regularly drink more than:

3-4 units per day

Women
Should not regularly drink more than:

2-3 units per day

In England there are:

25.9 million lower risk drinkers staying within the guidelines;

7.4 million increasing risk drinkers who regularly drink over the guideline amounts; and

2.6 million higher risk drinkers – men who regularly drink **over 8 units per day** and women who regularly drink **over 6 units per day**. They are at risk of becoming dependent on alcohol.

A significant proportion of people risk their health with excess drinking

Men

Percentage exceeding recommended level for weekly alcohol consumption, by age and gender, GB, 2010

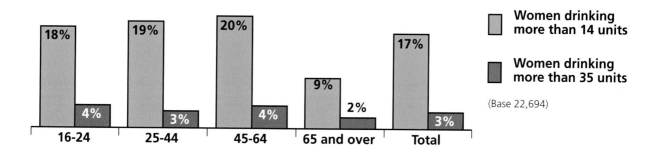

	16-24	25-44	45-64	65 and over	Total
Men drinking more than 21 units	21%	27%	30%	20%	26%
Men drinking more than 50 units	6%	7%	7%	4%	6%

Men drinking more than 21 units

Men drinking more than 50 units

(Base 20,197)

Women

	16-24	25-44	45-64	65 and over	Total
Women drinking more than 14 units	18%	19%	20%	9%	17%
Women drinking more than 35 units	4%	3%	4%	2%	3%

Women drinking more than 14 units

Women drinking more than 35 units

(Base 22,694)

Excess alcohol causes or contributes to health problems such as: liver and kidney disease; cancer; pancreatitis; heart disease; high blood pressure; depression; stroke.

In 2010/11, in England, **198,900 hospital admissions** were diagnosed as caused by alcohol. This is up 2.1% on the previous year and 40% since 2003.

There were **1,168,300 admissions** for conditions related to alcohol.

In 2011 there were **167,764 prescription items** for drugs for the treatment of alcohol dependency.

The cost of these was **£2.49 million**.

Hospital admissions where primary diagnosis was due to alcohol, England, 2010/11

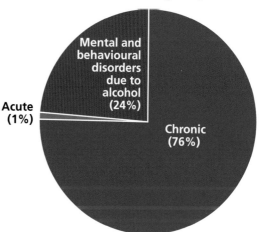

Mental and behavioural disorders due to alcohol (24%)

Acute (1%)

Chronic (76%)

Acute: appears quickly and can be serious or life-threatening
Chronic: persisting for a long period, often for the remainder of a person's lifetime

Sources: Alcohol Concern, Change4Life, Office for National Statistics © Crown copyright 2012
www.alcoholconcern.couldthisbe.com
www.nhs.uk/change4life
www.ons.gov.uk

SEE ALSO:
www.completeissues.co.uk

Drug highs

Many people have tried drugs but alcohol is the most popular stimulant

The largest ever survey on drug use was produced for Mixmag and the Guardian. Over 15,500 took part from Brazil to Birmingham, Phoenix to Finland

Who took the survey?

69.7% were male, **30.3%** were female, **82.7%** were heterosexual

78.2% were working, **39.5%** were (or were also) studying and **23.8%** were unemployed

The average age was **28 years and 4 months**, the most common age was **21**

What did they think?

76.2% said they **don't need drugs** for a good night out

68.4% agree or strongly agree with the statement **'drugs can make a good night out better'**

45.1% think drugs can make **a bad night out good**

In the UK, 7,700 people took part in the survey.
Percentage of UK respondents who HAD EVER TRIED the following:

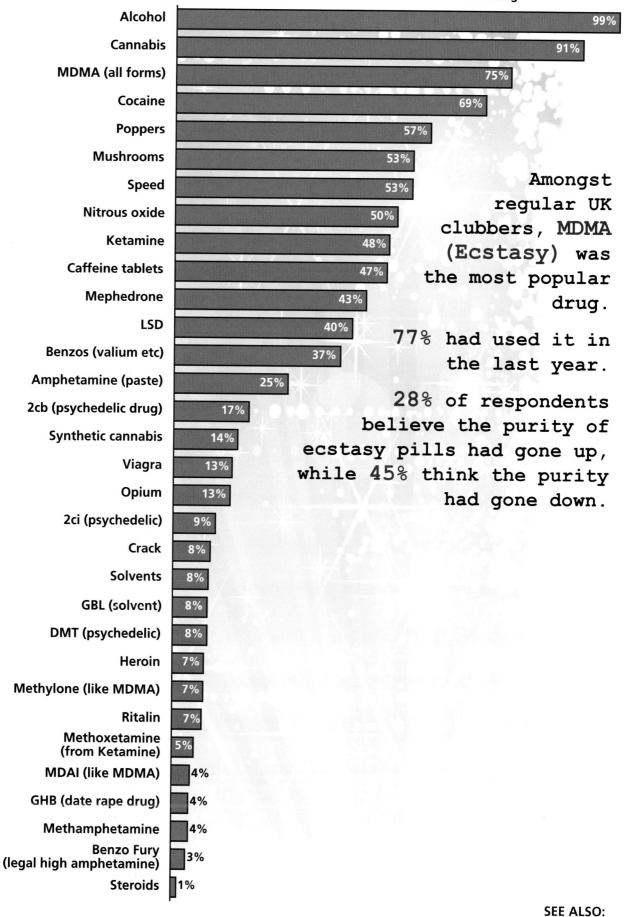

Drug	%
Alcohol	99%
Cannabis	91%
MDMA (all forms)	75%
Cocaine	69%
Poppers	57%
Mushrooms	53%
Speed	53%
Nitrous oxide	50%
Ketamine	48%
Caffeine tablets	47%
Mephedrone	43%
LSD	40%
Benzos (valium etc)	37%
Amphetamine (paste)	25%
2cb (psychedelic drug)	17%
Synthetic cannabis	14%
Viagra	13%
Opium	13%
2ci (psychedelic)	9%
Crack	8%
Solvents	8%
GBL (solvent)	8%
DMT (psychedelic)	8%
Heroin	7%
Methylone (like MDMA)	7%
Ritalin	7%
Methoxetamine (from Ketamine)	5%
MDAI (like MDMA)	4%
GHB (date rape drug)	4%
Methamphetamine	4%
Benzo Fury (legal high amphetamine)	3%
Steroids	1%

Amongst regular UK clubbers, MDMA (Ecstasy) was the most popular drug.

77% had used it in the last year.

28% of respondents believe the purity of ecstasy pills had gone up, while 45% think the purity had gone down.

Source: Mixmag / Guardian Drugs Survey, by Global Drug Survey
globaldrugsurvey.com

SEE ALSO:
Drug lows, p16-17
www.completeissues.co.uk

Drug lows

Despite worries and side effects, people still take drugs!

The largest ever survey on drug use was conducted by Mixmag and the Guardian.
Over 15,500 took part from Brazil to Birmingham, Phoenix to Finland

What drugs:

Of the 7,700 UK respondents who took part the most common stimulant for people to try was **alcohol** at **99%**. While this might not be a surprise, it is striking that **91%** had tried **cannabis**, **75%** had tried **MDMA (Ecstasy)** and **69%** had tried **cocaine**.

What worries you about your friends' drug use?

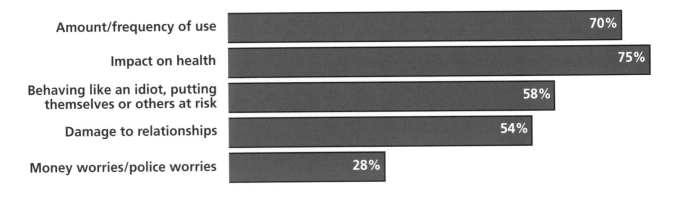

Amount/frequency of use	70%
Impact on health	75%
Behaving like an idiot, putting themselves or others at risk	58%
Damage to relationships	54%
Money worries/police worries	28%

Which substance are you most worried about your mates taking?

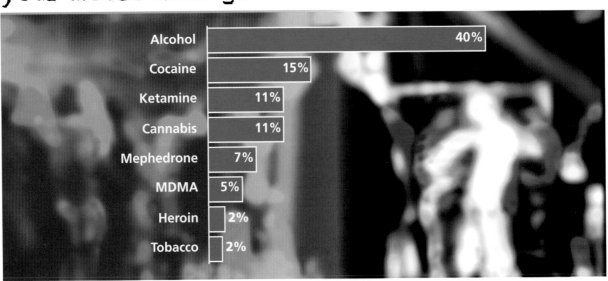

Alcohol	40%
Cocaine	15%
Ketamine	11%
Cannabis	11%
Mephedrone	7%
MDMA	5%
Heroin	2%
Tobacco	2%

Users of mephedrone, mdma and cocaine were asked which side-effects they had experienced either moderately or severely:

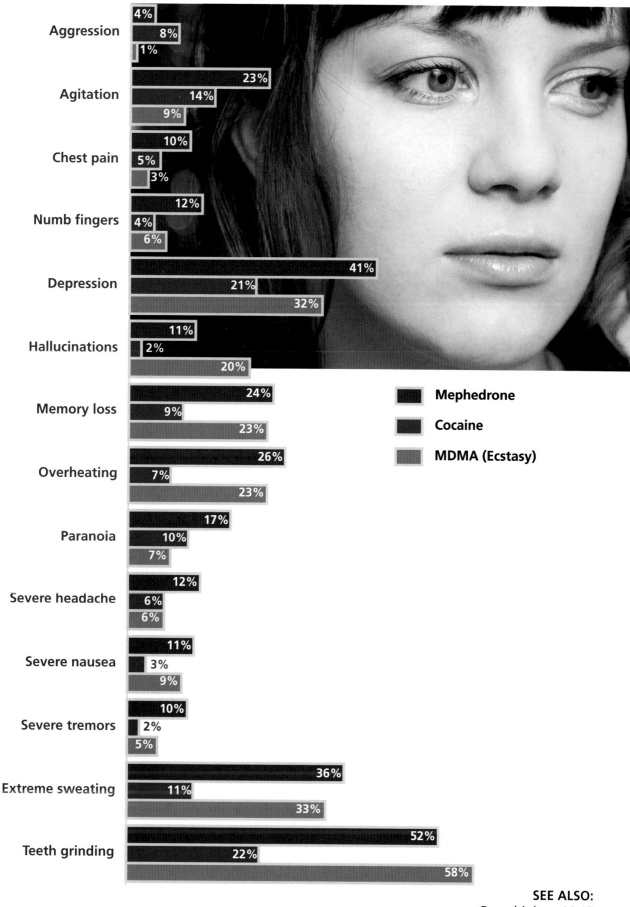

Aggression
- 4%
- 8%
- 1%

Agitation
- 23%
- 14%
- 9%

Chest pain
- 10%
- 5%
- 3%

Numb fingers
- 12%
- 4%
- 6%

Depression
- 41%
- 21%
- 32%

Hallucinations
- 11%
- 2%
- 20%

Memory loss
- 24%
- 9%
- 23%

Overheating
- 26%
- 7%
- 23%

Paranoia
- 17%
- 10%
- 7%

Severe headache
- 12%
- 6%
- 6%

Severe nausea
- 11%
- 3%
- 9%

Severe tremors
- 10%
- 2%
- 5%

Extreme sweating
- 36%
- 11%
- 33%

Teeth grinding
- 52%
- 22%
- 58%

■ Mephedrone
■ Cocaine
■ MDMA (Ecstasy)

Source: Mixmag / Guardian Drugs Survey, by Global Drug Survey
globaldrugsurvey.com

SEE ALSO:
Drug highs, p14-15
www.completeissues.co.uk

Temporary high

Although more than a third of adults have tried drugs, most people do not take them for long

All those aged 16-59 who said they had ever tried drugs were asked the age when they first tried the following drugs

(Base: 26,663 people)

% at each age

Legend:
- ■ Powder cocaine
- ▨ Ecstasy
- □ Cannabis

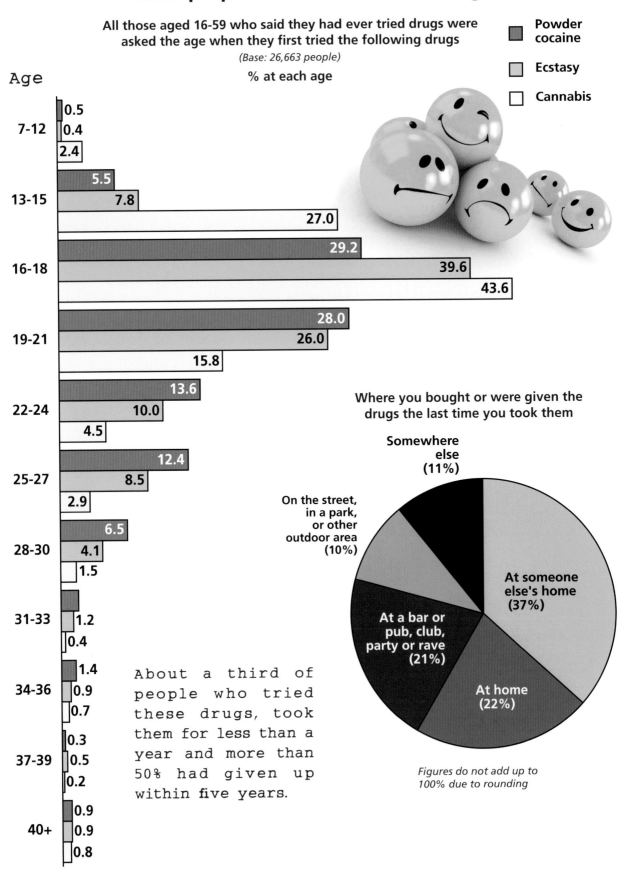

Age

7-12
- 0.5
- 0.4
- 2.4

13-15
- 5.5
- 7.8
- 27.0

16-18
- 29.2
- 39.6
- 43.6

19-21
- 28.0
- 26.0
- 15.8

22-24
- 13.6
- 10.0
- 4.5

25-27
- 12.4
- 8.5
- 2.9

28-30
- 6.5
- 4.1
- 1.5

31-33
- 1.2
- 0.4

34-36
- 1.4
- 0.9
- 0.7

37-39
- 0.3
- 0.5
- 0.2

40+
- 0.9
- 0.9
- 0.8

About a third of people who tried these drugs, took them for less than a year and more than 50% had given up within five years.

Where you bought or were given the drugs the last time you took them

- Somewhere else (11%)
- On the street, in a park, or other outdoor area (10%)
- At a bar or pub, club, party or rave (21%)
- At someone else's home (37%)
- At home (22%)

Figures do not add up to 100% due to rounding

Source: Crime Survey for England & Wales, Home Office
© Crown copyright 2012
www.crimesurvey.co.uk

SEE ALSO:
www.completeissues.co.uk

Animals

Acting for animals

The RSPCA continued to act against cruelty and neglect, with more convictions in 2011

The **Animal Welfare Act** was introduced in England and Wales in 2007, and has been described as the single most important piece of animal welfare legislation for nearly 100 years.

RSPCA Cruelty line
Tel: 0300 1234 999

1,314,795
phone calls received by the RSPCA – up **13%** from previous year

1,341
people convicted for cruelty and neglect to animals – up **23.5%**

2,105 convictions relating to cruelty to dogs – up **22%**

119,126
rescues & collections

159,759 complaints investigated

3,036 people reported to prosecutions department – up **9.3%**

1,100 bans imposed by the courts – up **21%**

74 prison sentences imposed by the courts – up **27%**

79,174 people given advice to improve animal welfare

Case studies:

Two men were *jailed* for 18 weeks and *banned* from keeping animals for life after they admitted causing a dog to *suffer unnecessarily*

———

Blind kitten found *dumped* in bag

———

Five pets left to die in *house of horror*

———

Ban after 37 dogs were removed

"We show zero tolerance to animal abusers. Anyone causing animals pain for profit or pleasure will be tracked down and prosecuted"
Gavin Grant
RSPCA chief executive

The RSPCA prosecution success rate for 2011:
98.2%

Pets were not the only victims – cases involving farm animals rose too

There were also **230** convictions relating to horses

Source: RSPCA
www.rspca.org.uk

SEE ALSO:
www.completeissues.co.uk

Animal research

The number of animals used for research is the highest for 25 years

Photo: courtesy of Understanding Animal Research

More than 3.79 million scientific procedures were carried out on animals in Great Britain in 2011

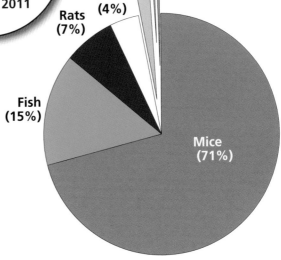

Types of animals used in experiments, Great Britain 2011

Other rodents (0.5%)

Reptiles/ amphibians (0.5%)

Other mammals (2%)

Birds (4%)

Rats (7%)

Fish (15%)

Mice (71%)

Why do we need animals in research?

Humans share at least 90% of their genes with every other mammal, and have the same vital organs, ie heart, lungs, liver, kidneys and brain.

The law says that animals cannot be used if medical research or testing can be done by a non-animal method but all potential medicines for humans must be safety-tested on animals first

Does it hurt the animals?

Lab animals are protected from cruelty during testing by law. All labs have regular inspections to make sure that testing is being carried out properly.

Does it work?

Animal research has been used to control diabetes, asthma and high blood pressure and has been used to develop antibiotics, vaccines, anaesthetics and blood transfusions.

But animals may respond to a drug differently to a human which can cause stress to the animal and affect the test result.

What are the alternatives?

- Taking tissue samples from humans and testing the drugs on them in a test tube
- Carrying out experiments using computer models and programmes
- Looking at large numbers of statistics

There were **increases** in the number of procedures for several species, eg

cats	+26%
pigs	+37%
birds	+14%
fish	+15%

and **decreases** for other species, eg

rats	-11%
guinea pigs	-16%
dogs	-21%
non-human primates	-47%

Areas of research

Animals are used in five main areas of medical research and product testing:

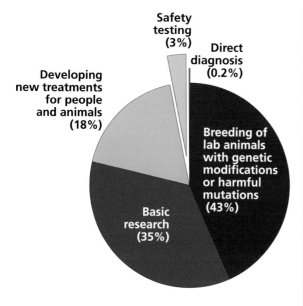

- Safety testing (3%)
- Direct diagnosis (0.2%)
- Developing new treatments for people and animals (18%)
- Breeding of lab animals with genetic modifications or harmful mutations (43%)
- Basic research (35%)

NB other purposes amounting to less than 1% of the total include education, training and forensic enquiries

Proportion of procedures by genetic status of lab animals

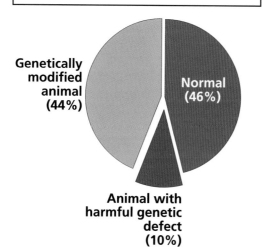

- Genetically modified animal (44%)
- Normal (46%)
- Animal with harmful genetic defect (10%)

Breeding of genetically modified (GM) animals and those with a harmful genetic defect, mainly mice, accounted for **1.62 million** procedures

Safety testing makes up a very small proportion of animal research – the wide range of chemicals which are used in everyday life such as medicines or household products as well as chemicals used in manufacturing, fertilisers and pesticides used in farming must be tested to make sure they are as safe as possible for animals and people.

Safety testing of ingredients in cosmetics and toiletries on animals has not been allowed since 1998.

Which products are tested on animals?

Some companies and shops offer products that have not been tested on animals. They often put information about this on their website. You can also write and ask the makers of your favourite products for more information.

> From January 2013 the suffering experienced by each animal has to be assessed and reported after each experiment. Previously the researcher had to estimate before the experiment how much suffering might be caused.
>
> *RSPCA*

Source: Statistics of Scientific Procedures on Living Animals – Home Office © Crown copyright 2012; Understanding Animal Research; RSPCA; BBC Newsround
www.homeoffice.gov.uk
www.understandinganimalresearch.org.uk
www.rspca.org.uk
www.bbc.co.uk/newsround

SEE ALSO:
www.completeissues.co.uk

Pet population

Britain isn't the only nation of pet lovers – or even the biggest

There are

240,805,900

pets in Europe

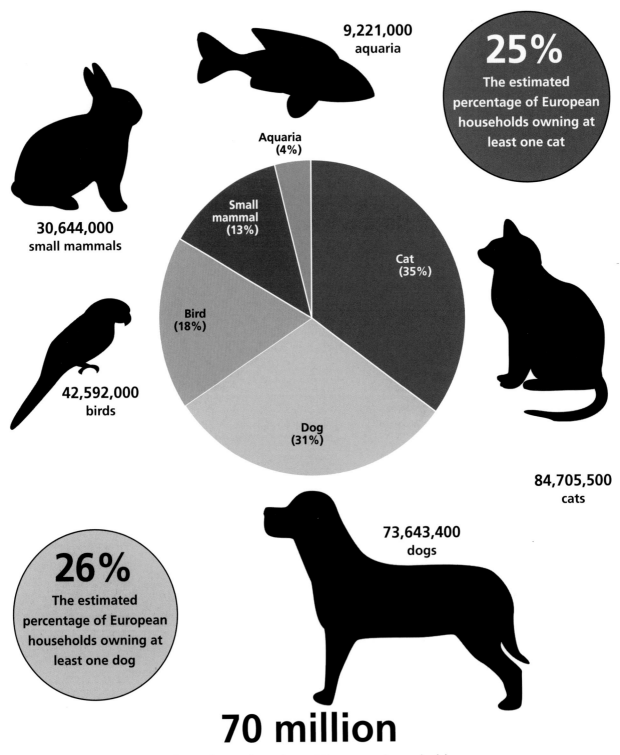

9,221,000
aquaria

25%
The estimated percentage of European households owning at least one cat

30,644,000
small mammals

Aquaria
(4%)

Small
mammal
(13%)

Cat
(35%)

Bird
(18%)

42,592,000
birds

Dog
(31%)

84,705,500
cats

73,643,400
dogs

26%
The estimated percentage of European households owning at least one dog

70 million

The estimated number of European households
(excluding Russia) owning at least one pet animal

European households owning at least one cat or one dog

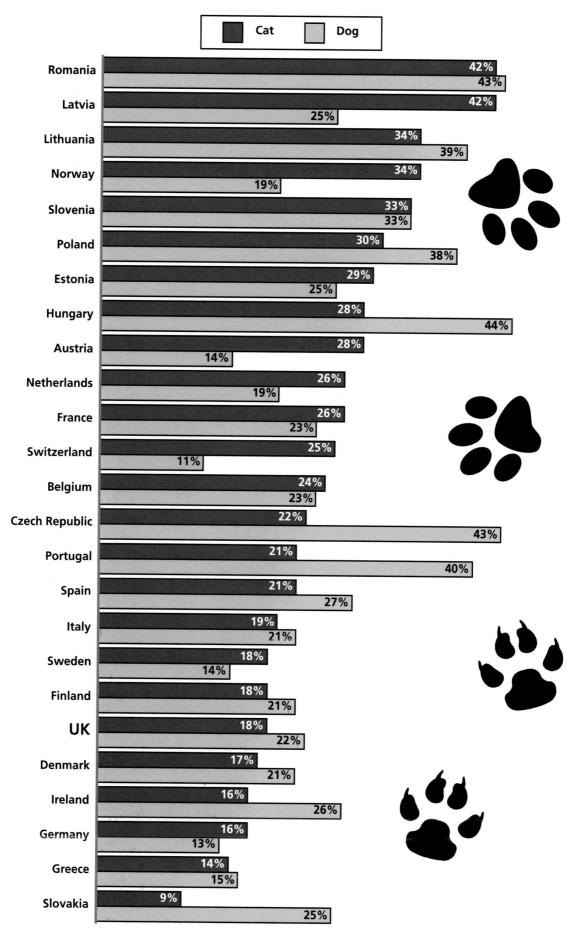

Country	Cat	Dog
Romania	42%	43%
Latvia	42%	25%
Lithuania	34%	39%
Norway	34%	19%
Slovenia	33%	33%
Poland	30%	38%
Estonia	29%	25%
Hungary	28%	44%
Austria	28%	14%
Netherlands	26%	19%
France	26%	23%
Switzerland	25%	11%
Belgium	24%	23%
Czech Republic	22%	43%
Portugal	21%	40%
Spain	21%	27%
Italy	19%	21%
Sweden	18%	14%
Finland	18%	21%
UK	18%	22%
Denmark	17%	21%
Ireland	16%	26%
Germany	16%	13%
Greece	14%	15%
Slovakia	9%	25%

Source: FEDIAF – The European Pet Food
Industry, Facts & Figures 2010
www.fediaf.org

SEE ALSO:
www.completeissues.co.uk

Wish you were here

Brits miss pets more than family when on holiday!

An online survey of 2,010 adult UK pet owners aged 18+ found that:

32% said they would rather go away with their pets than their immediate family.

10% would take their pet on holiday rather than the children, if they had the opportunity.

47% of those travelling without their family said it is their pet that they miss most of all while they're away.

39% chose to take their pets away with them on holiday either in the UK or abroad

Of those who took their pet on holiday **73%** said they didn't do it just for their own benefit – they believed their pet enjoyed the experience!

Pets were never far from their thoughts when they went on holiday

43% gave their pet extra TLC when they returned home.

18% made sure they brought back a souvenir for their pet.

40% said they regularly check on their pet whilst away to make sure they're ok.

36% their pet's welfare is their biggest worry when they do leave them behind.

Source: Opinium Research for TravelSupermarket.com
www.travelsupermarket.com
www.opinium.co.uk

SEE ALSO:
www.completeissues.co.uk

Britain & its citizens

Great outdoors?

Modern youngsters lack a variety of simple life skills which older generations take for granted

npower surveyed 1,000 children aged 5-13 and 1,000 parents in Britain.

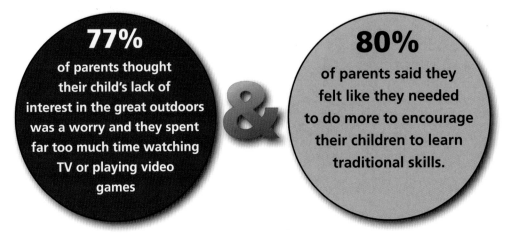

77% of parents thought their child's lack of interest in the great outdoors was a worry and they spent far too much time watching TV or playing video games

&

80% of parents said they felt like they needed to do more to encourage their children to learn traditional skills.

Things children aged 5-13 **CAN** do

67% could work a dvd player

58% could log on to the internet

50% play computer games on games console (wii, Xbox or similar)

46% make a phone call

45% use a handheld games console (Nintendo DSi, PSP or similar)

42% use an iPhone (or smartphone)

41% work Sky Plus

37% Search for clips on YouTube

31% use an iPad (or tablet computer)

38% send a text message

Things children aged 5-13 **CAN'T** do

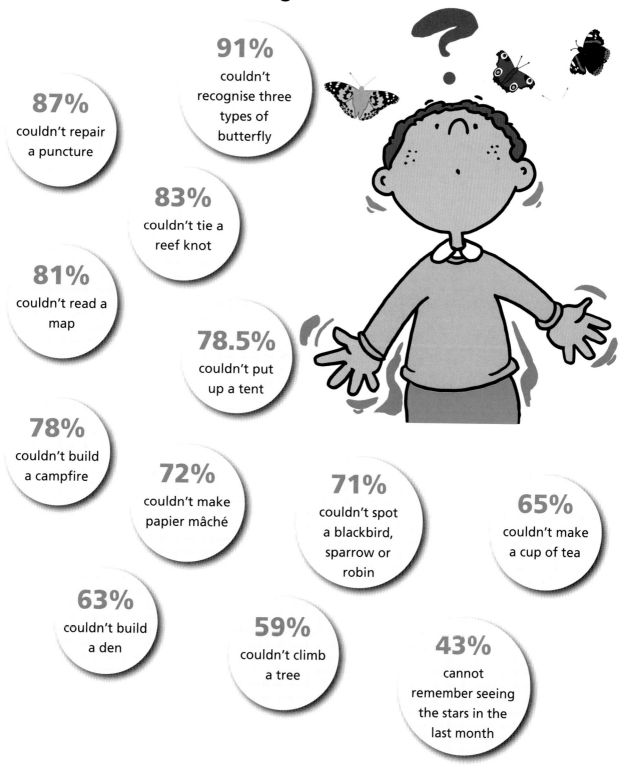

91% couldn't recognise three types of butterfly

87% couldn't repair a puncture

83% couldn't tie a reef knot

81% couldn't read a map

78.5% couldn't put up a tent

78% couldn't build a campfire

72% couldn't make papier mâché

71% couldn't spot a blackbird, sparrow or robin

65% couldn't make a cup of tea

63% couldn't build a den

59% couldn't climb a tree

43% cannot remember seeing the stars in the last month

" *simple skills like putting up a tent can teach you important lessons...* *you learn how to work in a team and communicate with your peers,* *how to work under pressure and use logic and most importantly* *how to look after yourself and know your strengths* "

Ray Mears, Survival Expert

Source: npower
www.npowermediacentre.com/

SEE ALSO:
www.completeissues.co.uk

Scoring a century!

Around one-third of babies born in 2012 in the UK are expected to live to celebrate their 100th birthday

Number of people aged 100 years (Centenarians), by gender, 1961 to 2010, UK

■ Females
■ Males

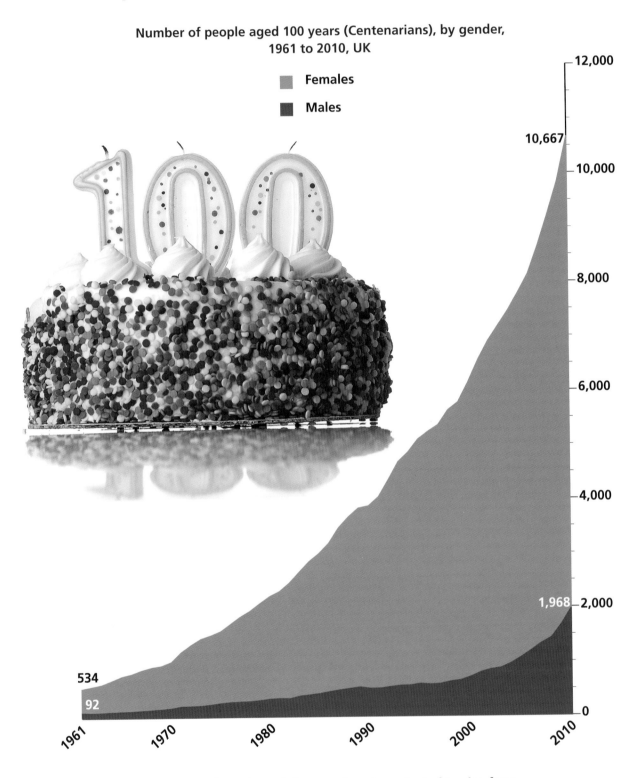

12,000

10,667

10,000

8,000

6,000

4,000

1,968 — 2,000

534

92

0

1961   1970   1980   1990   2000   2010

The total number of Centenarians is projected to rise from
14,500 in 2012 to **110,000** in 2035

39% of baby girls born in 2012 are expected to reach 100
compared with **32%** of baby boys.

What are your chances of reaching your 100th birthday?

**Projected numbers of people surviving to their
100th birthday by their age in 2012, UK**

The variations are based on current mortality rates –
deaths per 1,000 of the population

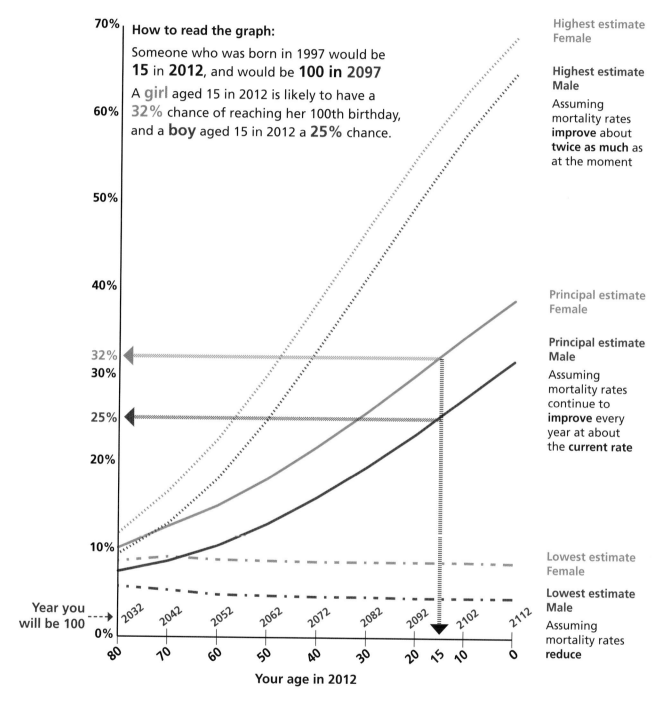

How to read the graph:

Someone who was born in 1997 would be
15 in **2012**, and would be **100 in 2097**

A girl aged 15 in 2012 is likely to have a
32% chance of reaching her 100th birthday,
and a **boy** aged 15 in 2012 a **25%** chance.

**Highest estimate
Female**

**Highest estimate
Male**

Assuming
mortality rates
improve about
twice as much as
at the moment

**Principal estimate
Female**

**Principal estimate
Male**

Assuming
mortality rates
continue to
improve every
year at about
the **current rate**

**Lowest estimate
Female**

**Lowest estimate
Male**

Assuming
mortality rates
reduce

Year you
will be 100

Your age in 2012

For those aged 20 and under their 100th birthday will not be
reached until 2092 or later – this means that 80 or more years
of assumptions are included in this calculation.

Source: Office for National Statistics © Crown copyright 2012
www.ons.gov.uk

SEE ALSO:
www.completeissues.co.uk

Alright?

Generally, people are content with how they live their lives

Q.1 All things considered, how satisfied are you with your life as a whole nowadays?
0 means extremely dissatisfied and 10 means extremely satisfied....

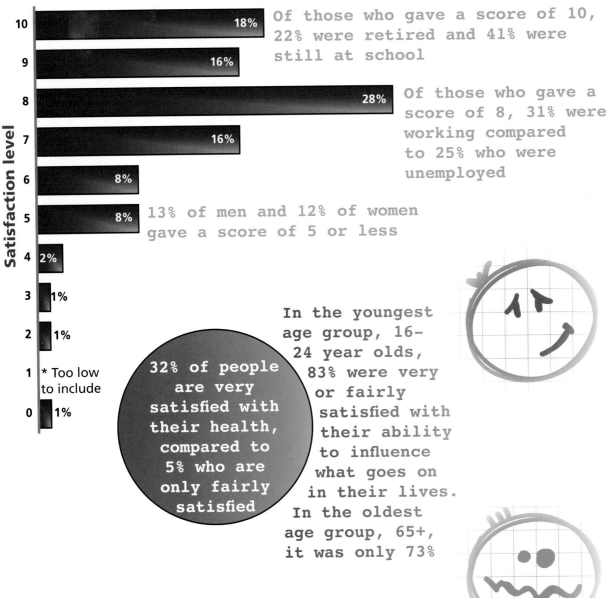

Satisfaction level

10	18%
9	16%
8	28%
7	16%
6	8%
5	8%
4	2%
3	1%
2	1%
1	* Too low to include
0	1%

Of those who gave a score of 10, 22% were retired and 41% were still at school

Of those who gave a score of 8, 31% were working compared to 25% who were unemployed

13% of men and 12% of women gave a score of 5 or less

32% of people are very satisfied with their health, compared to 5% who are only fairly satisfied

In the youngest age group, 16-24 year olds, 83% were very or fairly satisfied with their ability to influence what goes on in their lives. In the oldest age group, 65+, it was only 73%

Q.2 How satisfied are you with your standard of living?

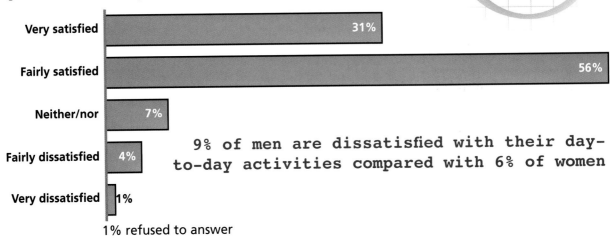

Very satisfied	31%
Fairly satisfied	56%
Neither/nor	7%
Fairly dissatisfied	4%
Very dissatisfied	1%

1% refused to answer

9% of men are dissatisfied with their day-to-day activities compared with 6% of women

Q.3 How satisfied are you with your personal relationships?

- Very satisfied — **51%**
- Fairly satisfied — **37%**
- Neither/nor — **7%**
- Fairly dissatisfied — **2%**
- Very dissatisfied — **1%**

1% refused to answer
1% didn't know

27% of those aged 16-24 were very satisfied about achieving their goals in life, compared with only 22% of those aged 65+

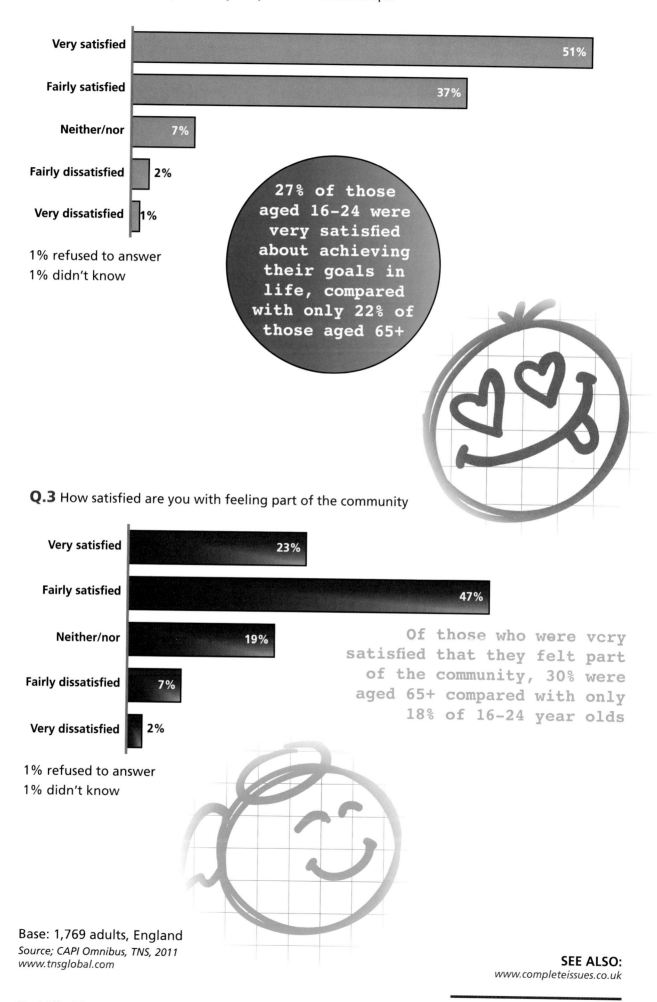

Q.3 How satisfied are you with feeling part of the community

- Very satisfied — **23%**
- Fairly satisfied — **47%**
- Neither/nor — **19%**
- Fairly dissatisfied — **7%**
- Very dissatisfied — **2%**

1% refused to answer
1% didn't know

Of those who were very satisfied that they felt part of the community, 30% were aged 65+ compared with only 18% of 16-24 year olds

Base: 1,769 adults, England

Source; CAPI Omnibus, TNS, 2011
www.tnsglobal.com

SEE ALSO:
www.completeissues.co.uk

Royal reception

Views about the Royals are generally positive

With major public events such as the Royal Wedding and the Diamond Jubilee more attention has been paid to the Royal Family and how we feel about them.

1,002 adults were asked people how they felt about the Monarchy.

Do you think Britain would be better off or worse off without a Royal Family?

Don't know (9%)

Better off (22%)

Worse off (69%)

Photo: Damian Herde / Shutterstock.com

When the Queen abdicates or dies, what do you think should happen next?

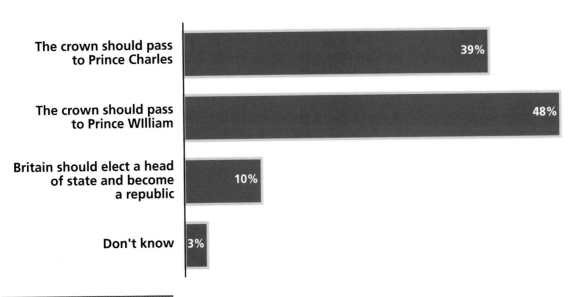

The crown should pass to Prince Charles — 39%

The crown should pass to Prince WIlliam — 48%

Britain should elect a head of state and become a republic — 10%

Don't know — 3%

In a different survey, 1,000 adults were asked about how they felt towards the Royal Family.

55% of people said that the **Royal Family** are either **important** or **very important** to British culture and society, compared to only **15%** who think they **aren't important**.

58% of people would describe their **opinion** of the **Royals** as **positive**.

Queen Elizabeth ranked highly – coming out as **favourite** Royal with those aged **55 and over**, and **second favourite** with **other age groups**.

The Queen's **Jubilee** celebrations were noted as one of the top reasons the public **felt warmer** towards the Royal Family.

Photo: Featureflash / Shutterstock.com

"The Queen remains dignified even in this age of celebrity."

"The Queen's status is that of an icon."

Photo: Featureflash / Shutterstock.com

Young Royals

The Young Royals such as **William, Harry and Kate** came out as top reason why the public feel optimistic towards the Monarchy with a huge **56%** of votes.

Although the **Queen** rated top with the older generation, overall the UK's favourite Royal is **Prince Harry** with **17%**, followed by the **Queen** with **15.9%**, **Prince William** with **15.6%**, and **Kate Middleton** with **12%**.

31% said they feel most proud to have **Queen Elizabeth** as British monarch – but **35%** would feel proudest with **William** as **King**. This is compared to a mere **6%** that chose **Prince Charles**, linking with the findings from the other poll that he should consider passing the role of **King** straight to **William** when he gains the crown.

Source: ICM opinion poll, 2012 and OnePoll Data Hub
www.icmresearch.com
news.onepoll.com

SEE ALSO:
www.completeissues.co.uk

Being British

What is Britishness...?

...could it be about accepting diversity and respecting cultures?

A Channel 4 Poll explored what it means to be British.

Q Which of the following would you say makes you most **PROUD** to be British?
(more than one answer could be given)

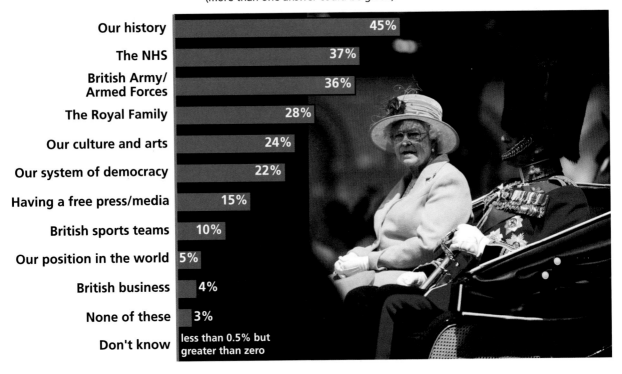

Our history	45%
The NHS	37%
British Army/Armed Forces	36%
The Royal Family	28%
Our culture and arts	24%
Our system of democracy	22%
Having a free press/media	15%
British sports teams	10%
Our position in the world	5%
British business	4%
None of these	3%
Don't know	less than 0.5% but greater than zero

Q Which of the following do you think **STOPS** people being fully British?
(more than one answer could be given)

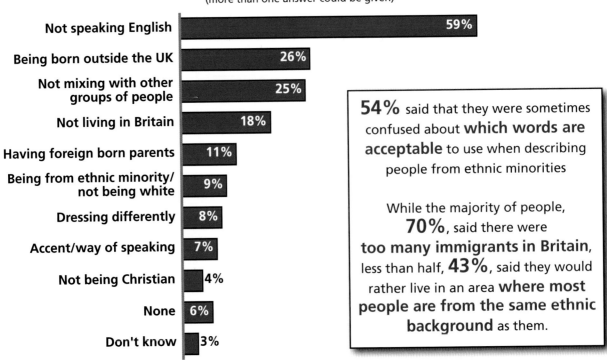

Not speaking English	59%
Being born outside the UK	26%
Not mixing with other groups of people	25%
Not living in Britain	18%
Having foreign born parents	11%
Being from ethnic minority/not being white	9%
Dressing differently	8%
Accent/way of speaking	7%
Not being Christian	4%
None	6%
Don't know	3%

54% said that they were sometimes confused about **which words are acceptable** to use when describing people from ethnic minorities

While the majority of people, **70%**, said there were **too many immigrants in Britain**, less than half, **43%**, said they would rather live in an area **where most people are from the same ethnic background** as them.

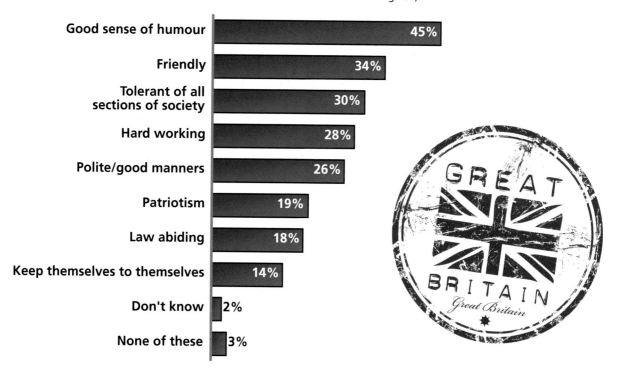

Q Which of the following do you think are the
BEST characteristics of British people?
(more than one answer could be given)

Good sense of humour	45%
Friendly	34%
Tolerant of all sections of society	30%
Hard working	28%
Polite/good manners	26%
Patriotism	19%
Law abiding	18%
Keep themselves to themselves	14%
Don't know	2%
None of these	3%

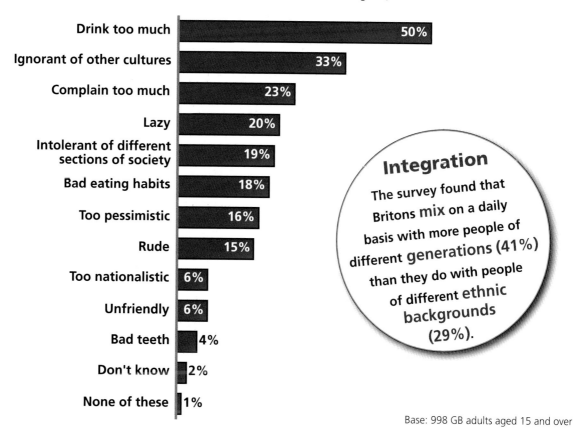

Q Which of the following do you think are the
WORST characteristics of British people?
(more than one answer could be given)

Drink too much	50%
Ignorant of other cultures	33%
Complain too much	23%
Lazy	20%
Intolerant of different sections of society	19%
Bad eating habits	18%
Too pessimistic	16%
Rude	15%
Too nationalistic	6%
Unfriendly	6%
Bad teeth	4%
Don't know	2%
None of these	1%

Integration

The survey found that Britons mix on a daily basis with more people of different generations (41%) than they do with people of different ethnic backgrounds (29%).

Base: 998 GB adults aged 15 and over

Source: Ipsos Mori for Channel 4, Joseph Rowntree Charitable Trust
www.ipsos-mori.com
www.channel4.com
www.jrf.org.uk

SEE ALSO:
www.completeissues.co.uk

Has Britain changed?

Have attitudes changed since the 1948 Olympics?

A poll contrasted the state of the nation in the Olympic year 2012 with 1948 – the last time the Olympics were held in Britain.

People were asked:

To what extent do you agree or disagree with the following statements about the way Britain has changed since 1948?

Agree

Neither/nor

Disagree

Don't know

Net figure
(the difference between those who agree and those who disagree. Figure is rounded)

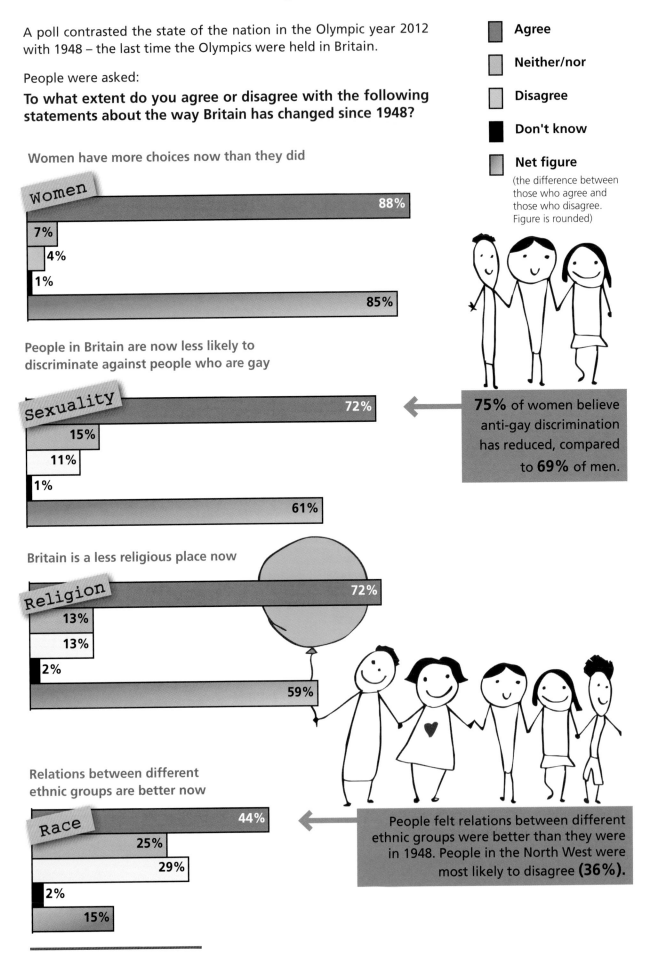

Women have more choices now than they did

Women
- 88%
- 7%
- 4%
- 1%
- 85%

People in Britain are now less likely to discriminate against people who are gay

Sexuality
- 72%
- 15%
- 11%
- 1%
- 61%

75% of women believe anti-gay discrimination has reduced, compared to **69%** of men.

Britain is a less religious place now

Religion
- 72%
- 13%
- 13%
- 2%
- 59%

Relations between different ethnic groups are better now

Race
- 44%
- 25%
- 29%
- 2%
- 15%

People felt relations between different ethnic groups were better than they were in 1948. People in the North West were most likely to disagree **(36%)**.

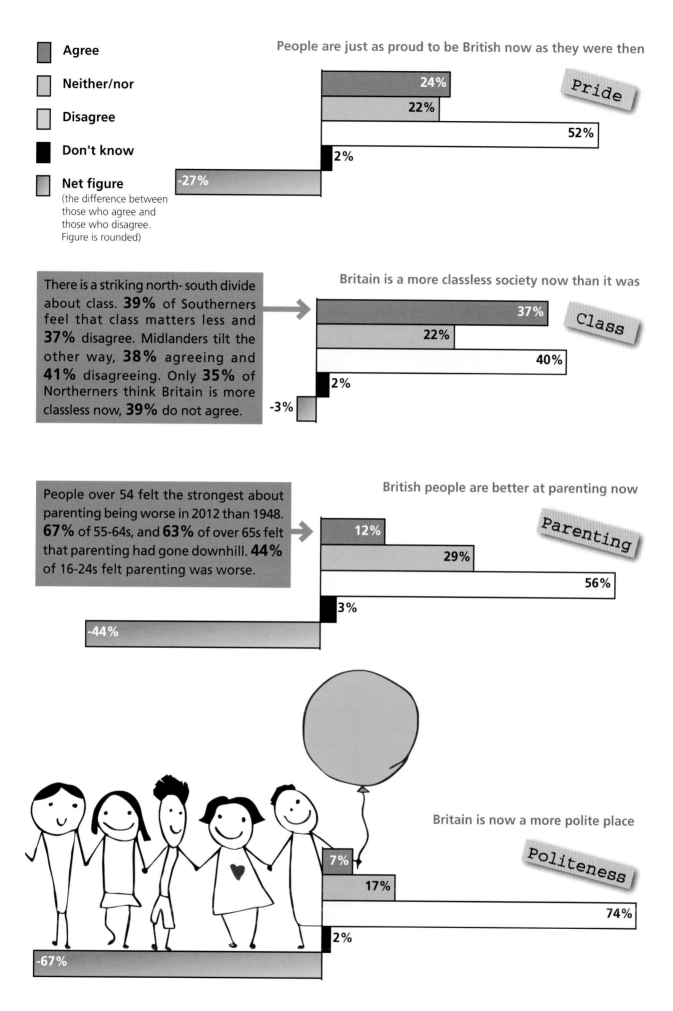

Agree

Neither/nor

Disagree

Don't know

Net figure
(the difference between
those who agree and
those who disagree.
Figure is rounded)

People are just as proud to be British now as they were then

Pride

24%

22%

52%

2%

-27%

There is a striking north-south divide about class. **39%** of Southerners feel that class matters less and **37%** disagree. Midlanders tilt the other way, **38%** agreeing and **41%** disagreeing. Only **35%** of Northerners think Britain is more classless now, **39%** do not agree.

Britain is a more classless society now than it was

Class

37%

22%

40%

2%

-3%

People over 54 felt the strongest about parenting being worse in 2012 than 1948. **67%** of 55-64s, and **63%** of over 65s felt that parenting had gone downhill. **44%** of 16-24s felt parenting was worse.

British people are better at parenting now

Parenting

12%

29%

56%

3%

-44%

Britain is now a more polite place

Politeness

7%

17%

74%

2%

-67%

Source: British Future State of the Nation,
Hopes and Fears 2012 poll
www.britishfuture.org

SEE ALSO:
www.completeissues.co.uk

Hopes and fears

The British public are concerned about the state of the country, but still have faith in family

What do you think are the biggest challenges Britain will face
(Combined score of issues ranked in the top three by all age groups)

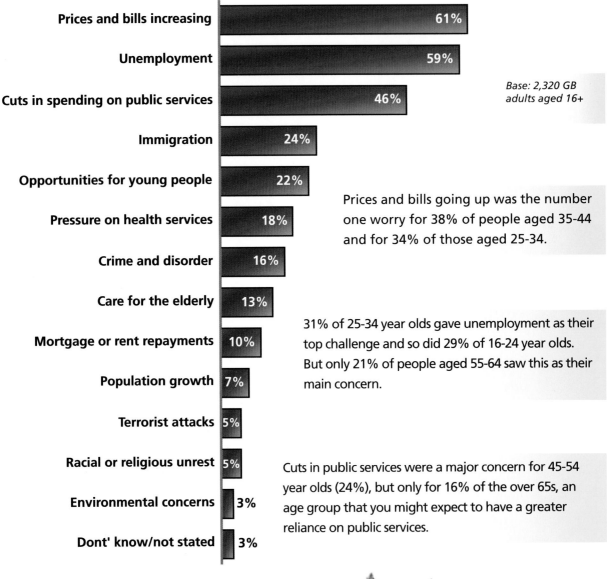

Prices and bills increasing	61%
Unemployment	59%
Cuts in spending on public services	46%
Immigration	24%
Opportunities for young people	22%
Pressure on health services	18%
Crime and disorder	16%
Care for the elderly	13%
Mortgage or rent repayments	10%
Population growth	7%
Terrorist attacks	5%
Racial or religious unrest	5%
Environmental concerns	3%
Dont' know/not stated	3%

Base: 2,320 GB adults aged 16+

Prices and bills going up was the number one worry for 38% of people aged 35-44 and for 34% of those aged 25-34.

31% of 25-34 year olds gave unemployment as their top challenge and so did 29% of 16-24 year olds. But only 21% of people aged 55-64 saw this as their main concern.

Cuts in public services were a major concern for 45-54 year olds (24%), but only for 16% of the over 65s, an age group that you might expect to have a greater reliance on public services.

Photo: Rosli Othman / Shutterstock.com

Men and women were asked if they felt optimistic about...

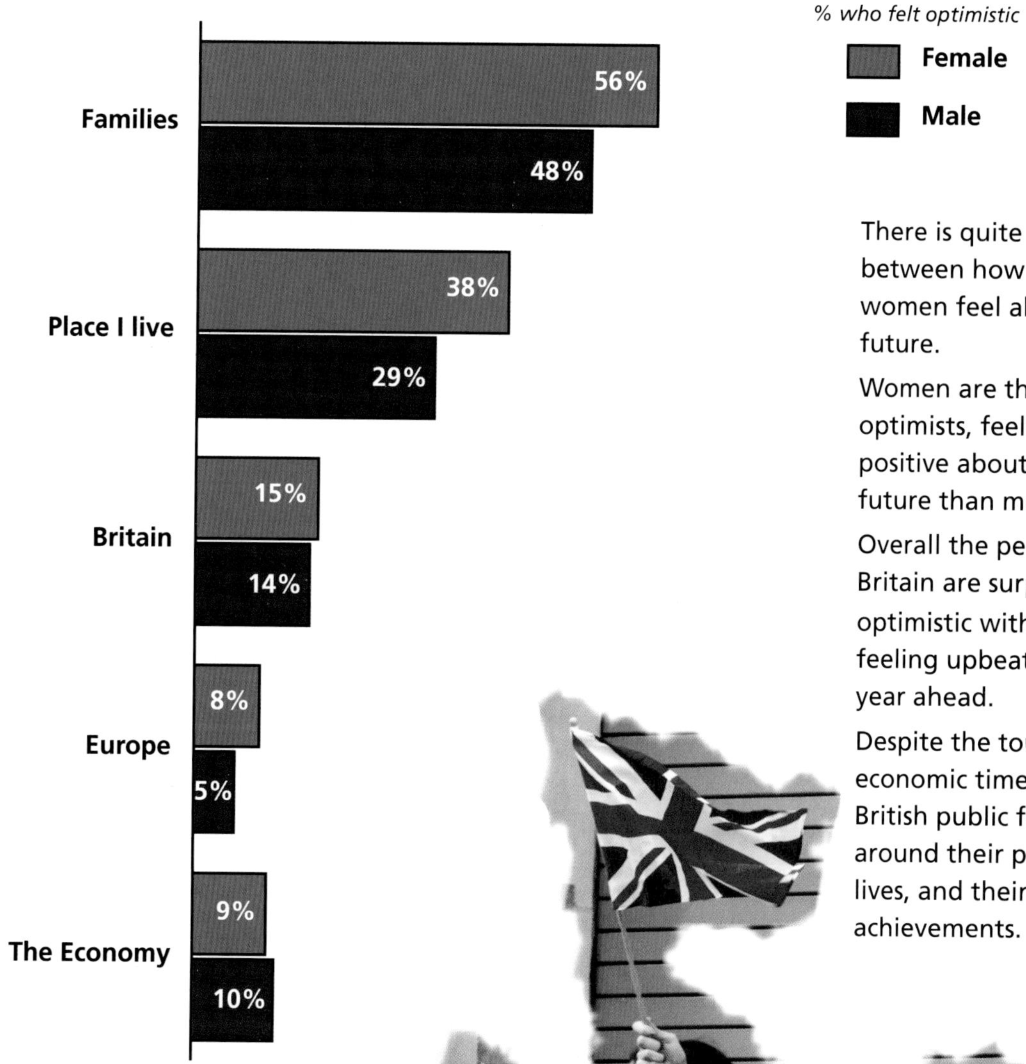

% who felt optimistic

Female
Male

Families
- 56%
- 48%

Place I live
- 38%
- 29%

Britain
- 15%
- 14%

Europe
- 8%
- 5%

The Economy
- 9%
- 10%

There is quite a difference between how men and women feel about the future.

Women are the nation's optimists, feeling more positive about their future than men.

Overall the people in Britain are surprisingly optimistic with 52% feeling upbeat about the year ahead.

Despite the tough economic times, the British public feel upbeat around their personal lives, and their family's achievements.

Photo: Phil Jones / Shutterstock.com

Source: British Future State of the Nation, Hopes and Fears 2012 poll
www.britishfuture.org

SEE ALSO:
www.completeissues.co.uk

Worried nation

The number of people calling Samaritans about money worries has doubled since the financial downturn

20% of people contacting Samaritans in 2011 talked about **job concerns, housing problems, debt** and other **financial pressures**.

Job security and redundancy had been worrying both unemployed people, **41%**, and those working full time, **36%**.

58% feared they wouldn't have enough money to live comfortably in the coming year

36% were concerned about losing their job or having difficulty finding work.

These issues are reflected in the Samaritan's annual survey of the nation's worries

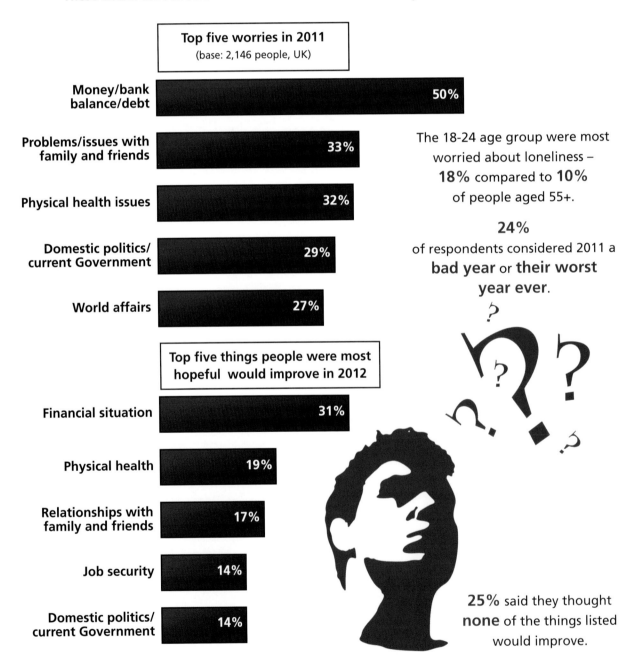

Top five worries in 2011
(base: 2,146 people, UK)

Worry	%
Money/bank balance/debt	50%
Problems/issues with family and friends	33%
Physical health issues	32%
Domestic politics/current Government	29%
World affairs	27%

The 18-24 age group were most worried about loneliness – **18%** compared to **10%** of people aged 55+.

24% of respondents considered 2011 a **bad year** or **their worst year ever**.

Top five things people were most hopeful would improve in 2012

Thing	%
Financial situation	31%
Physical health	19%
Relationships with family and friends	17%
Job security	14%
Domestic politics/current Government	14%

25% said they thought **none** of the things listed would improve.

Source: Samaritans; YouGov
www.samaritans.org
www.yougov.co.uk

SEE ALSO:
www.completeissues.co.uk

Charity

Global giving

The world is giving less money but more time to charity

The World Giving Index surveys over 150,000 people in 153 countries, which represents around **95%** of the world's population.

They were asked about three aspects of giving: **Have you done any of the following in the past month?**

- **Donated money** to a charity
- **Volunteered your time** to an organisation
- **Helped a stranger**, or someone you didn't know who needed help

The survey averages the responses from the three key questions, each country is given a percentage and then ranked in order based on their score.

Top 10 most giving nations, 2011 World Giving Index overall % score	2011 ranking	2010 ranking
USA — 60%	1st	5th
Ireland — 59%	2nd	=3rd
Australia — 58%	3rd	=1st
New Zealand — 57%	=4th	=1st
UK — 57%	=4th	=8th
Netherlands — 54%	=6th	7th
Canada — 54%	=6th	=3rd
Sri Lanka — 51%	=8th	=8th
Thailand — 51%	=8th	25th
Lao People's Democratic Republic — 50%	10th	11th

The countries whose populations are most likely to give are not necessarily the world's most wealthy

The **increase** in giving is due to more **helping strangers** – up **2%** – and more **volunteering time** – **1%**. But the **giving of money has fallen** by **1%**.

Although the increase in scores is small, an increase of even **1%** is equivalent to hundreds of thousands of people behaving differently.

Giving means very different things across the different continents

Countries ranked 1-5, by the % of the population giving money

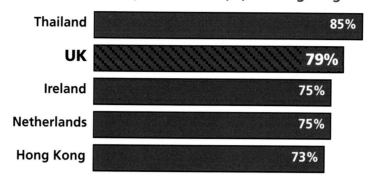

Country	%
Thailand	85%
UK	79%
Ireland	75%
Netherlands	75%
Hong Kong	73%

Countries ranked 1-5, by the % of the population volunteering time

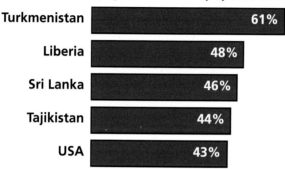

Country	%
Turkmenistan	61%
Liberia	48%
Sri Lanka	46%
Tajikistan	44%
USA	43%

UK ranks 32nd with 28% volunteering time

Countries ranked 1-5, by the % of the population helping a stranger

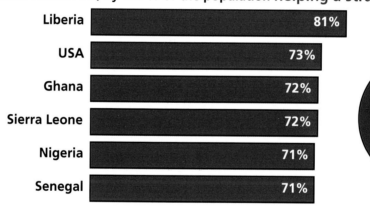

Country	%
Liberia	81%
USA	73%
Ghana	72%
Sierra Leone	72%
Nigeria	71%
Senegal	71%

UK ranks 17th with 63% helping a stranger

Giving money to charity and **volunteering time** are both growing fastest amongst the **oldest age groups.**

Helping strangers is becoming more common amongst those of **middle age.**

Thanks! Danke! Gracias! Grazie! Merci! Toda! Efcharisto!

Source: World Giving Index 2011, Charities Aid Foundation
www.cafonline.org

SEE ALSO:
www.completeissues.co.uk

Giving matters

More people in the UK are giving to charity but they are giving smaller amounts

In 2010/11 the percentage of people giving increased slightly over the last year from **56%** to **58%**, suggesting that giving has returned to pre-recession levels. The amount typically given in a month was **£11** per person, down from £12 the previous year.

In general, charitable giving has remained steady over the past seven years since the survey began, which indicates that it is a well-established behaviour. The only exception was 2008/09 when giving dipped, probably owing to the recession.

In 2010/11, almost **60%** of adults donated to charitable causes in a typical month.

The total amount donated to charity was around **£11 billion.**

Percentage of donors, by amount given, 2010/11
Base: 3,000 UK adults aged 16 years and over

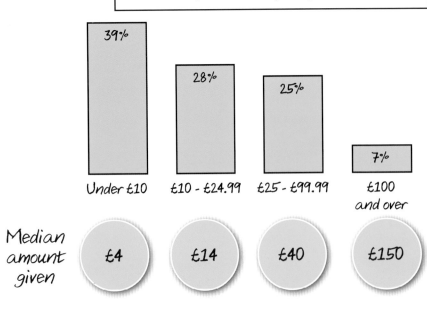

	Under £10	£10 - £24.99	£25 - £99.99	£100 and over
Percentage	39%	28%	25%	7%
Median amount given	£4	£14	£40	£150

Although the proportion of donors giving more than £100 is small, their donations account for a large share of the total amount donated – **45%** of the total.

This doesn't take into account donations from the very wealthy – it is estimated in a typical year there are around **100 donations** worth **£1m** or more made by individual donors.

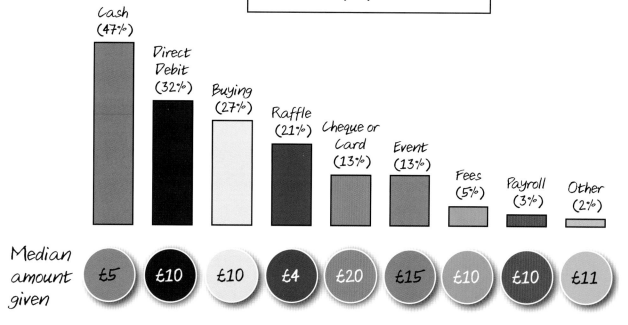

The method people use to donate

Cash (47%)
Direct Debit (32%)
Buying (27%)
Raffle (21%)
Cheque or Card (13%)
Event (13%)
Fees (5%)
Payroll (3%)
Other (2%)

Median amount given: £5 £10 £10 £4 £20 £15 £10 £10 £11

Although **cash** is the most popular method of giving, because each donation is smaller it doesn't provide the biggest income.

Which method generates most money?

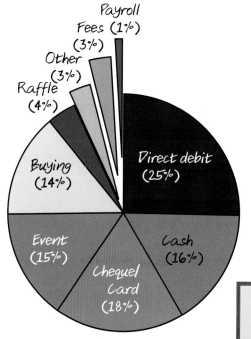

Payroll (1%)
Fees (3%)
Other (3%)
Raffle (4%)
Buying (14%)
Event (15%)
Chequel Card (18%)
Cash (16%)
Direct debit (25%)

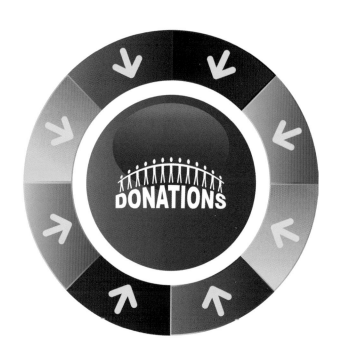

The fact that so many people freely choose to give, to support the huge range of causes that matter to them, is a very positive reflection on our society.

UK Giving 2011

Source: UK Giving 2011 – National Council for Voluntary Organisations (NCVO) and Charities Aid Foundation (CAF)
www.ncvo-volorg.uk
www.cafonline.org

SEE ALSO:
www.completeissues.co.uk

Givers ...

The youngest adults are the least likely to give

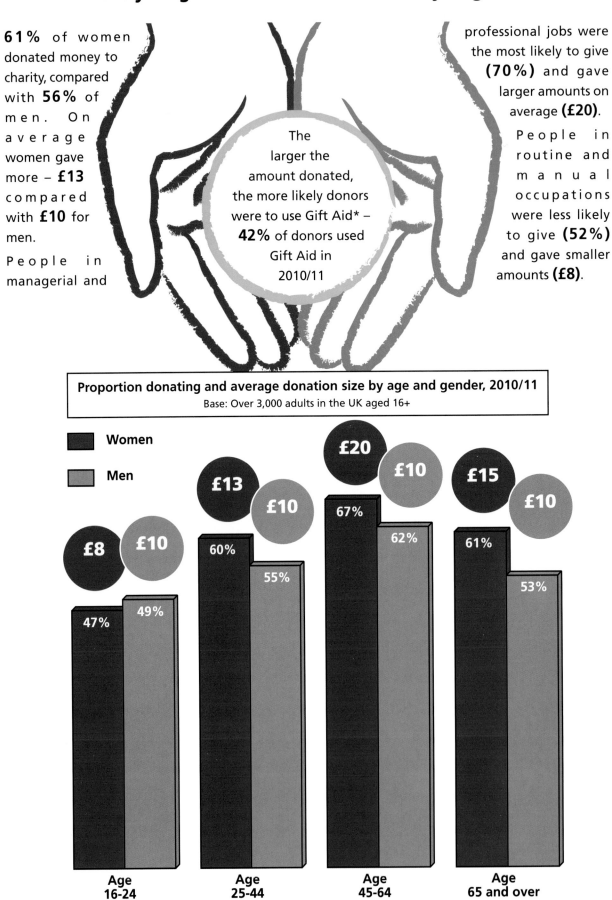

61% of women donated money to charity, compared with **56%** of men. On average women gave more – **£13** compared with **£10** for men.

People in managerial and

The larger the amount donated, the more likely donors were to use Gift Aid* – **42%** of donors used Gift Aid in 2010/11

professional jobs were the most likely to give **(70%)** and gave larger amounts on average **(£20)**.

People in routine and manual occupations were less likely to give **(52%)** and gave smaller amounts **(£8)**.

Proportion donating and average donation size by age and gender, 2010/11
Base: Over 3,000 adults in the UK aged 16+

Women

Men

£8 **£10**

£13 **£10**

£20 **£10**

£15 **£10**

47% 49%

60% 55%

67% 62%

61% 53%

Age 16-24

Age 25-44

Age 45-64

Age 65 and over

*Gift Aid allows donors to increase the value of their donation by allowing the charity to reclaim the tax on the money.

... and receivers

Medical research has always been the best-supported cause

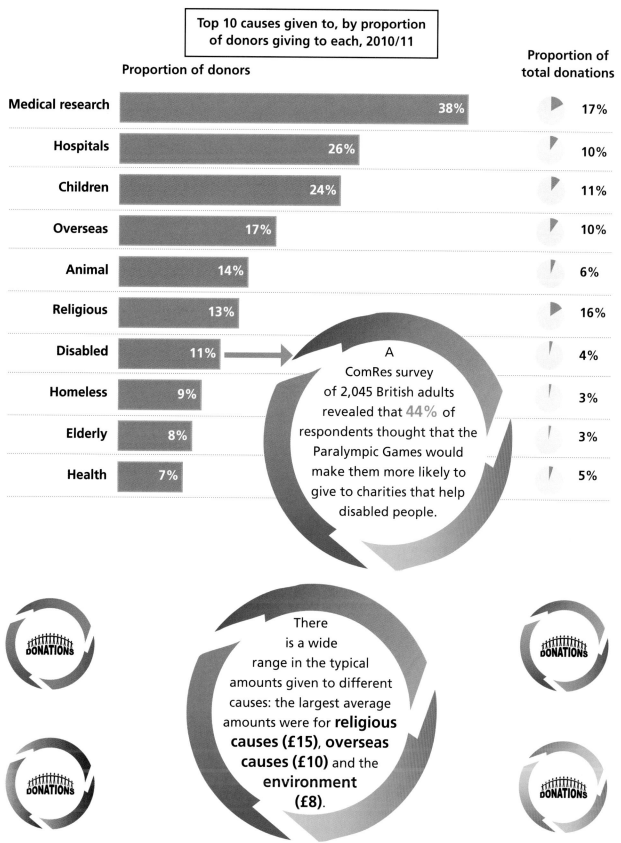

Top 10 causes given to, by proportion of donors giving to each, 2010/11

Proportion of donors

Cause	Proportion of donors	Proportion of total donations
Medical research	38%	17%
Hospitals	26%	10%
Children	24%	11%
Overseas	17%	10%
Animal	14%	6%
Religious	13%	16%
Disabled	11%	4%
Homeless	9%	3%
Elderly	8%	3%
Health	7%	5%

A ComRes survey of 2,045 British adults revealed that 44% of respondents thought that the Paralympic Games would make them more likely to give to charities that help disabled people.

There is a wide range in the typical amounts given to different causes: the largest average amounts were for **religious causes (£15), overseas causes (£10)** and the **environment (£8)**.

Source: UK Giving 2011 – National Council for Voluntary Organisations and Charities Aid Foundation; ComRes
www.ncvo-volorg.uk
www.cafonline.org
www.comres.co.uk

SEE ALSO:
www.completeissues.co.uk

Choose charity shops

Charity shops are a uniquely British institution... but they can't survive without donations from the public

Warren Alexander, Chief Executive of the Charity Retail Association

Charity shop **income** is at an **all time high** of nearly **£1 billion** and **£30 million more** was spent in British charity shops in the last year, representing a **3.6% growth** over the year.

The British public are relying on charity shops to get through the recession

Over the last year, **1 million** more people from struggling middle class groups were shopping in charity shops.

22% said that they were shopping in charity shops **more frequently** now than two years ago.

19% of existing customers say they would buy even more from charity shops in the next year.

Mothers of young children depended on charity shops for basic necessities.

73% of mothers who had shopped in charity shops in the past year had bought items for their children and **55%** bought children's clothes.

50% of those surveyed who were **affected by child benefit cuts** are shopping in charity shops **more frequently** than two years ago.

© Howard Lake, Flickr

Why not donate?

15% of people who **didn't donate** said it was because they **couldn't afford to** buy new clothing so were **keeping things for longer**.

31% of mothers and **one in 6** of those surveyed admitted they had started to **sell** their unwanted clothes to make money **instead of donating them**.

Base: A survey of 3,600 charity shops and 1,822 UK consumers

Source: Charity Retail Association; JRA Consumer Research
www.charityretail.org.uk
www.jraresearch.com
www.choosecharityshops.org

SEE ALSO:
www.completeissues.co.uk

Education

Priced out?

**University applications have fallen.
Is the rise in tuition fees to blame?**

From 2012, universities in **England** can charge up to **£9,000** per year for undergraduate courses, raising the cap from its 2011/12 level of £3,375.

From 2012, Scottish universities will be able to charge up to £9,000 for students from elsewhere in the UK but Students from **Scotland** attending Scottish universities **do not pay fees**.

Welsh universities can charge fees of up to £9,000, but the Welsh Assembly will pay fees above **£3,465** a year for Welsh students studying at any UK university.

At universities in **Northern Ireland**, tuition fees for students from Northern Ireland in 2012 will be capped at **£3,465**.

Number of applicants for university per year

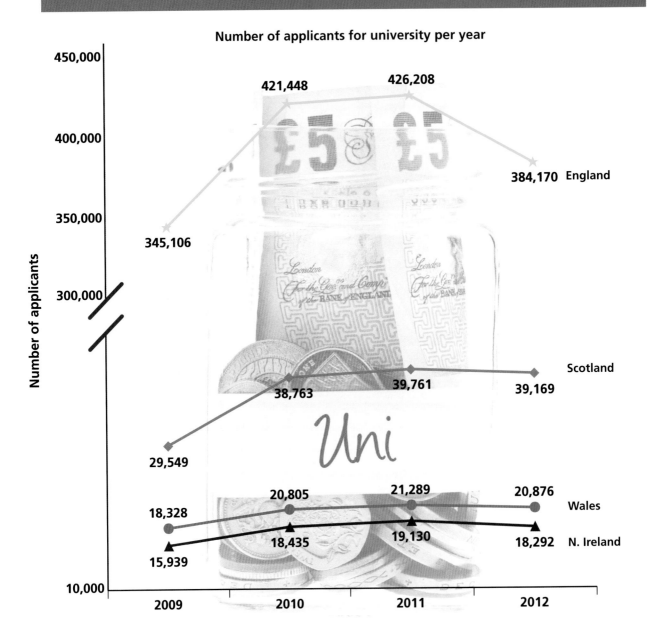

Number of applicants

450,000

421,448

426,208

400,000

384,170 England

350,000

345,106

300,000

Scotland

38,763   39,761   39,169

29,549

20,805   21,289   20,876

18,328   Wales

18,435   19,130   18,292 N. Ireland

15,939

10,000

2009   2010   2011   2012

Applications peaked in all areas in 2011, the last year before the introduction of increased fees. Comparing 2010 figures to 2012 reflects people's choices before and after the announcement about increased fees. In 2012 applications across the **UK** were down by **7.4%** compared to 2010, in **England** they were **down by 8.8%**

In April 2012, students in Years 10 to 13 in English schools were asked:

To what extent has the increase in university tuition fees influenced your decision to apply to a university in the UK?

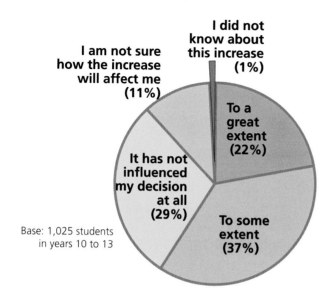

I am not sure how the increase will affect me (11%)

I did not know about this increase (1%)

It has not influenced my decision at all (29%)

To a great extent (22%)

To some extent (37%)

Base: 1,025 students in years 10 to 13

Will you apply to go to university?

Year 13

had not applied (23%)

had applied (77%)

unsure either way (10%)

Year 10-12

very or fairly unlikely (16%)

very or fairly likely (74%)

This small group of students in years 10-13 who were not applying was asked:

Please select the three main reasons you would not apply to university

The **top five reasons** were:

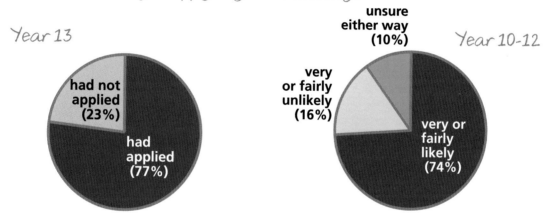

Tuition fees	74%
Overall cost	71%
Rather have a job/career	50%
Exam results	34%
My family can't/won't support me	32%

NB: The small size of the sample means the results should be treated with caution

Sources: Independent commission on fees, Analysis of UCAS applications for 2012/13 admissions; NFER Pupil Voice Survey of students about university entrance, April 2012
www.ucas.com
www.nfer.ac.uk

SEE ALSO:
www.completeissues.co.uk

Falling support

How much public support is there for young people in higher education?

In 2011 **47%** of young people were participating in Higher Education. But as the number of places has increased, public support for the policy appears to have diminished.

Trends in views on the level of higher education participation, 2002-2007 and 2010

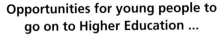

Opportunities for young people to go on to Higher Education ...

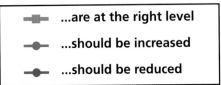

- ...are at the right level
- ...should be increased
- ...should be reduced

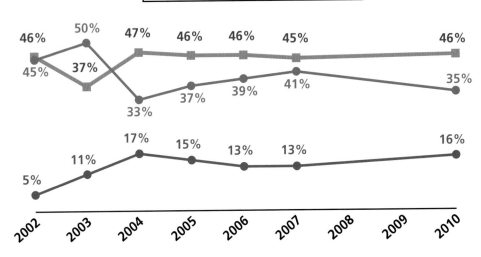

Twice as many people want an increase in places, than want a reduction.

However, graduates are much more likely to support a reduction in the number of university places than people who have no formal qualifications

Percentage saying Higher Education opportunities should be reduced, by educational level, 2010

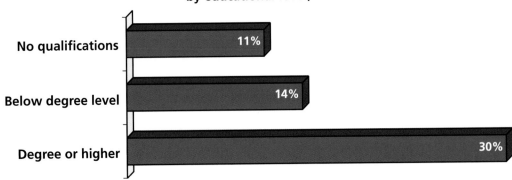

No qualifications	11%
Below degree level	14%
Degree or higher	30%

NB Figures throughout are England only, since the situation on fees is different for students whose family home is in England from those who live in Scotland, Wales and Northern Ireland

Attitudes towards student finance may also be changing

People were asked what they thought about

university or college students or their families paying towards the cost of their tuition, either while they are studying or after they have finished.

Who should pay toward tuition costs?
(NB: the question was asked before the rise in tuition fees to a maximum of £9,000)

70%
Some students/ families should pay

13%
All students/ families should pay

16%
No students/ families should pay

People were told:

Many full time university students are now taking out government loans to help cover their living costs

and asked whether students should or should not be expected to take out loans.

Should students be expected to take out loans?

14%
it depends

42%
should not be expected to

43%
should be expected to

NB: Totals may not add up to 100% due to rounding

Source: British Social Attitudes 28, NatCen Social Research
www.natcen.ac.uk

SEE ALSO:
www.completeissues.co.uk

Grade expectations

A fall in GCSE grades has caused concern and controversy

The proportion of GCSEs awarded an A*-C grade fell for the first time in 2012. When the exams were introduced in 1988, **42.5%** of entries were awarded an A-C grade. This has risen every year until it reached **69.8%** in **2011**.

Percentage of GCSE entrants receiving grades A/A* to C, UK

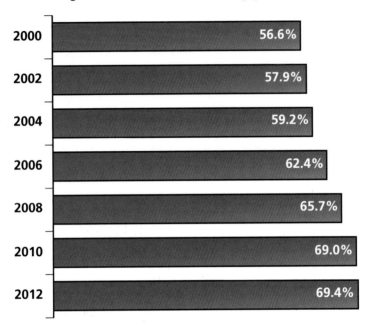

Year	Percentage
2000	56.6%
2002	57.9%
2004	59.2%
2006	62.4%
2008	65.7%
2010	69.0%
2012	69.4%

	Percentage of GCSE entrants receiving grades A*/A	Proportion receiving A*
2000	15.8%	4.6%
2002	16.4%	5.0%
2004	17.4%	5.6%
2006	19.1%	6.3%
2008	20.7%	6.8%
2010	22.6%	7.5%
2012	22.4%	7.3%

In 2012 there was a decrease in the proportion of GCSEs at least at Grade C in the core subjects of maths, science and English.

Why this matters:

For the schools – they must achieve 40% of pupils with five good GCSEs including English and Maths or risk closure or conversion to academies.

For the pupils – a Grade C in these core subjects is often essential for entry into A/S courses, college, university and apprenticeships.

The English Controversy

One of the three elements of this qualification was coursework completed under exam conditions. It was possible to complete this at different times. Those pupils who submitted their coursework in June 2011 or January 2012 needed **55 marks out of 96** to achieve **Grade C**. Those who did the same work in June 2012 needed **64 marks out of 96** to achieve the same grade.

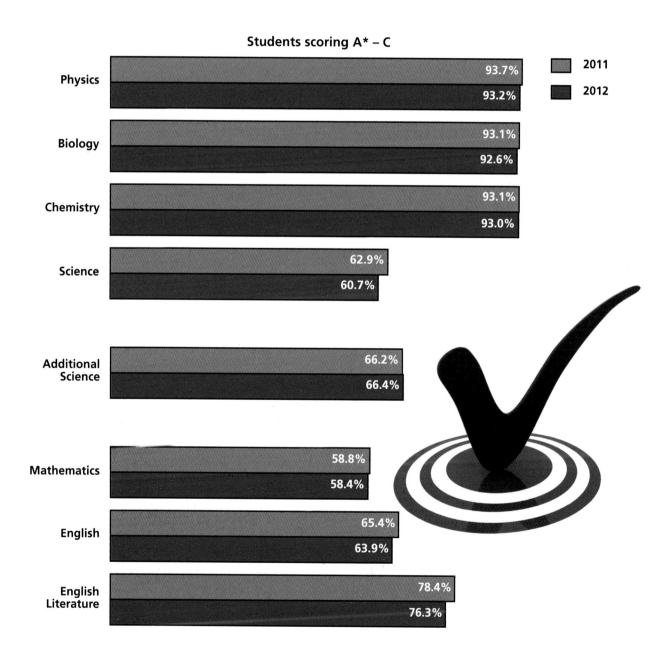

Students scoring A* – C

Subject	2011	2012
Physics	93.7%	93.2%
Biology	93.1%	92.6%
Chemistry	93.1%	93.0%
Science	62.9%	60.7%
Additional Science	66.2%	66.4%
Mathematics	58.8%	58.4%
English	65.4%	63.9%
English Literature	78.4%	76.3%

Source: Joint Council for Qualifications
www.jcq.org.uk

SEE ALSO:
Top marks, p58-59
www.completeissues.co.uk

Top marks

A level grades and subjects

Percentage of A level entrants receiving pass grades, (A-E), UK

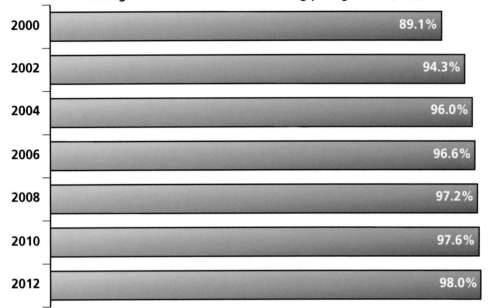

Year	Percentage
2000	89.1%
2002	94.3%
2004	96.0%
2006	96.6%
2008	97.2%
2010	97.6%
2012	98.0%

The overall A level pass rate has risen again for the 30th year with 98% of entrants achieving at least a Grade E...

...but there has been a fall in the proportion of A-levels awarded an A or A* grade for the first time in over 20 years.

Percentage of A level entrants receiving grades A*/A, UK

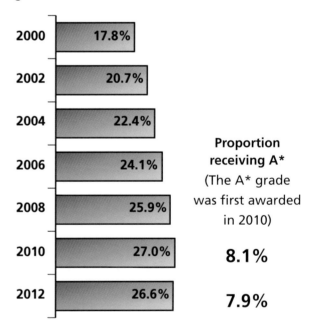

Year	Percentage	Proportion receiving A*
2000	17.8%	
2002	20.7%	
2004	22.4%	
2006	24.1%	
2008	25.9%	
2010	27.0%	8.1%
2012	26.6%	7.9%

Proportion receiving A*
(The A* grade was first awarded in 2010)

Exam boards say that the slight fall in top grades awarded was probably related to a different make-up of students this year: there are fewer 18-year-olds in the population but more of them did A-levels, so the ability-range is wider.

50% of entries in independent schools achieved A* or A grade, compared to 23% in state schools and colleges.

Most popular subjects at A level, by percentage of entrants

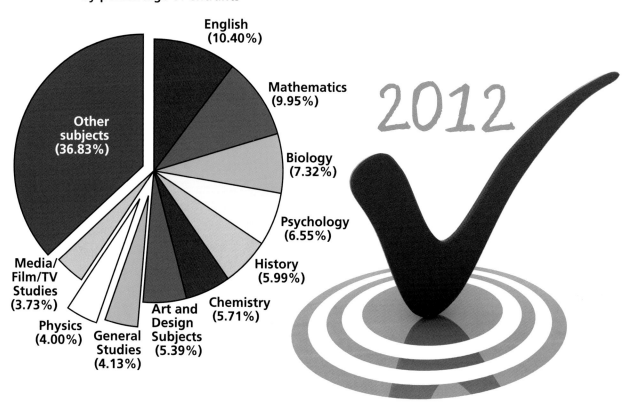

- English (10.40%)
- Mathematics (9.95%)
- Biology (7.32%)
- Psychology (6.55%)
- History (5.99%)
- Chemistry (5.71%)
- Art and Design Subjects (5.39%)
- General Studies (4.13%)
- Physics (4.00%)
- Media/Film/TV Studies (3.73%)
- Other subjects (36.83%)

2012

Subjects with the highest percentage of A* grades

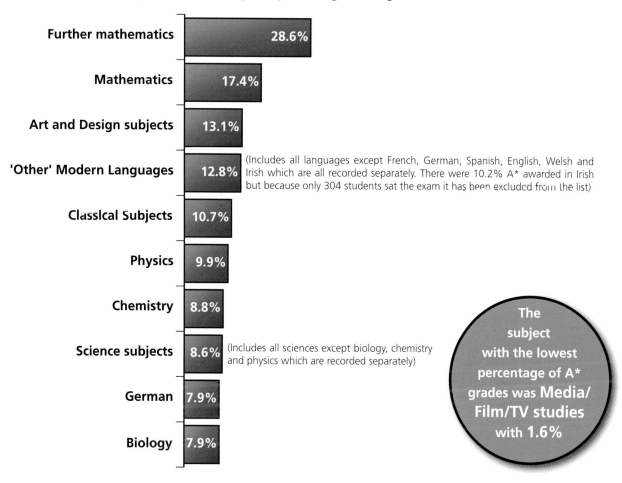

Subject	Percentage
Further mathematics	28.6%
Mathematics	17.4%
Art and Design subjects	13.1%
'Other' Modern Languages	12.8%
Classical Subjects	10.7%
Physics	9.9%
Chemistry	8.8%
Science subjects	8.6%
German	7.9%
Biology	7.9%

'Other' Modern Languages: (Includes all languages except French, German, Spanish, English, Welsh and Irish which are all recorded separately. There were 10.2% A* awarded in Irish but because only 304 students sat the exam it has been excluded from the list)

Science subjects: (Includes all sciences except biology, chemistry and physics which are recorded separately)

The subject with the lowest percentage of A* grades was Media/Film/TV studies with 1.6%

Source: Joint Council for Qualifications
www.jcq.org.uk

SEE ALSO:
Grade expectations, p56-57

www.completeissues.co.uk

Levelling out

More young people are achieving higher levels of education – but achievement isn't equal across all social groups

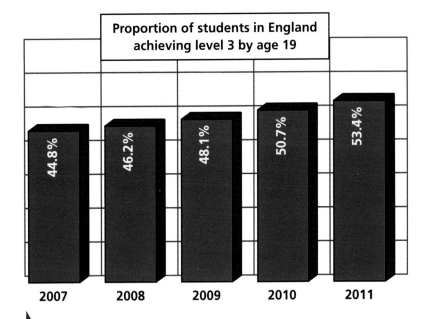

Proportion of students in England achieving level 3 by age 19

- 2007: 44.8%
- 2008: 46.2%
- 2009: 48.1%
- 2010: 50.7%
- 2011: 53.4%

Level 3 Qualifications include:

A levels, GCE in applied subjects, International Baccalaureate, Key Skills level 3, BTEC level 3, BTEC Nationals, OCR Nationals, NVQs at level 3

Eligibility for Free School Meals (FSM) is taken as a rough indicator of relative deprivation. Although more students in this category are achieving level 3, so are the rest of their age group and the **achievement gap between the two groups has reduced by just 1% over 5 years.**

Proportion of 19 year olds qualified to level 3, by FSM uptake

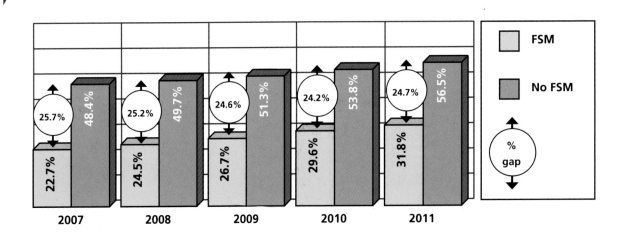

Year	FSM	% gap	No FSM
2007	22.7%	25.7%	48.4%
2008	24.5%	25.2%	49.7%
2009	26.7%	24.6%	51.3%
2010	29.6%	24.2%	53.8%
2011	31.8%	24.7%	56.5%

When deprivation is measured more widely, the effect of social background can be seen.

General deprivation can be measured across 7 categories: income, employment, health and disability, education, skills and training, barriers to housing and services, living environment and crime

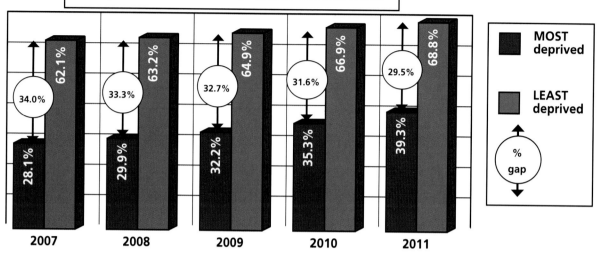

Proportion of students in England achieving level 3 Comparison between LEAST and MOST DEPRIVED

	2007	2008	2009	2010	2011
MOST deprived	28.1%	29.9%	32.2%	35.3%	39.3%
LEAST deprived	62.1%	63.2%	64.9%	66.9%	68.8%
% gap	34.0%	33.3%	32.7%	31.6%	29.5%

Ethnic background also appears to have a bearing on attainment

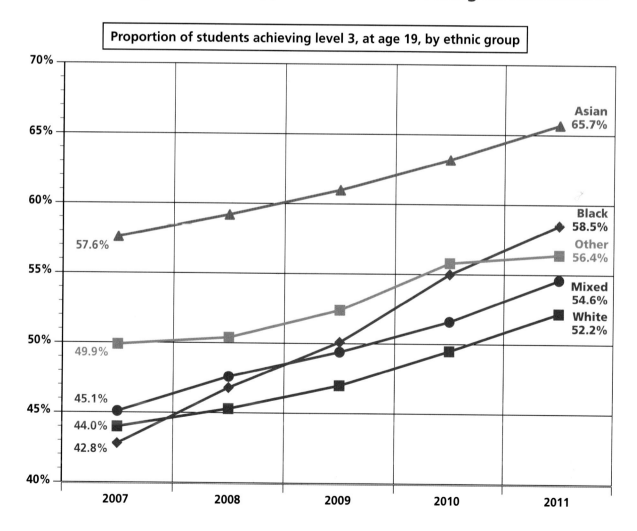

Proportion of students achieving level 3, at age 19, by ethnic group

Asian 65.7%
Black 58.5%
Other 56.4%
Mixed 54.6%
White 52.2%

57.6%
49.9%
45.1%
44.0%
42.8%

Source: Department for Education © Crown copyright 2012
www.education.gov.uk

SEE ALSO:
www.completeissues.co.uk

Skipping school

Pupil absence rates have fallen – is this a result of harsher penalties for parents?

Persistent absence is defined as missing 15% of school days – equal to skipping a month's worth of lessons in a year.

Percentage of pupils that are persistent absentees in secondary schools

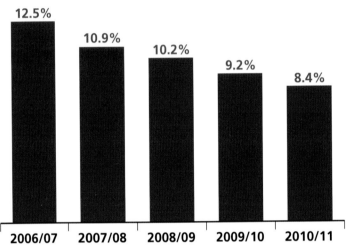

2006/07	2007/08	2008/09	2009/10	2010/11
12.5%	10.9%	10.2%	9.2%	8.4%

Percentage of pupils that are persistent absentees in secondary schools, by ethnic group, 2010/11

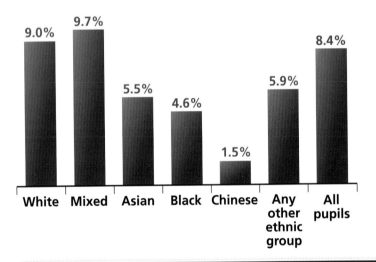

White	Mixed	Asian	Black	Chinese	Any other ethnic group	All pupils
9.0%	9.7%	5.5%	4.6%	1.5%	5.9%	8.4%

There is only a small difference in persistent absence between boys and girls.

However there are high rates amongst:

- pupils eligible for Free School Meals – **18.3%**
- Year 11 pupils – **12.6%** (in contrast to **4.9%** in Year 7)
- pupils with Special Educational Needs – **15.1%**.

If children are persistently absent from school their parents can be given a penalty notice of £50 to £100 pounds. Parents can also be prosecuted - resulting in a fine of up to £2,500, a community order or even a jail sentence. Alternatively a Parenting Order can require them to attend parenting education classes.

Source: Pupil Absence in Schools in England, 2010/11
© Crown copyright 2012
www.education.gov.uk

SEE ALSO:
www.completeissues.co.uk

Environmental Issues

Force of nature

Natural disasters caused devastation in 101 countries in 2011

Natural Disaster: an unforeseen and often sudden event that causes great damage, destruction and human suffering eg flooding or earthquake	Disaster types	Examples
	Climatological events caused by long term climate processes	Extreme temperature, drought, wildfire
	Geophysical events originating from solid earth	Earthquake, volcano, rockfall
	Hydrological events caused by abnormal water behaviour	Flood, avalanches, landslides
	Meteorological events caused by short term weather processes	Storms

Top 10 countries by number of reported events, 2011

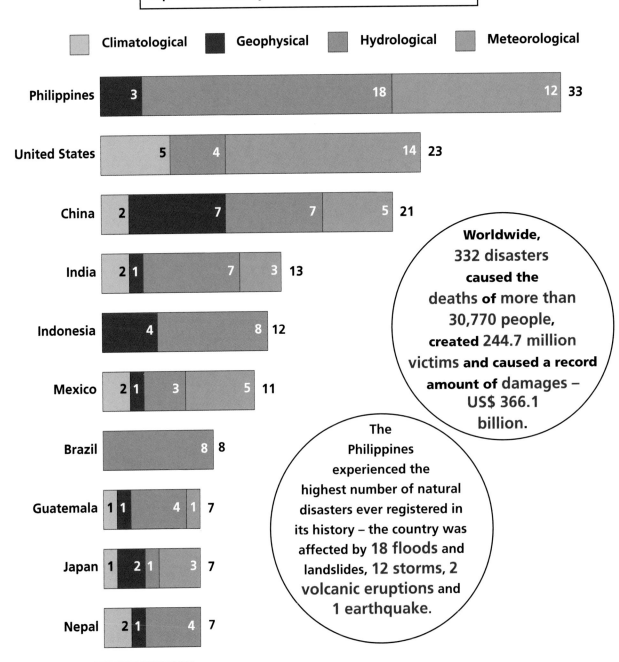

Climatological   Geophysical   Hydrological   Meteorological

Philippines: 3 | 18 | 12 — 33
United States: 5 | 4 | 14 — 23
China: 2 | 7 | 7 | 5 — 21
India: 2 | 1 | 7 | 3 — 13
Indonesia: 4 | 8 — 12
Mexico: 2 | 1 | 3 | 5 — 11
Brazil: 8 — 8
Guatemala: 1 | 1 | 4 | 1 — 7
Japan: 1 | 2 | 1 | 3 — 7
Nepal: 2 | 1 | 4 — 7

Worldwide, 332 disasters caused the deaths of more than 30,770 people, created 244.7 million victims and caused a record amount of damages – US$ 366.1 billion.

The Philippines experienced the highest number of natural disasters ever registered in its history – the country was affected by 18 floods and landslides, 12 storms, 2 volcanic eruptions and 1 earthquake.

The five countries that were most often hit – the **Philippines**, the **US**, **China**, **India** and **Indonesia**, accounted for **31%** of all disasters.

The Tōhoku earthquake and tsunami in **Japan** on 11th March 2011 recorded **64.5%** of worldwide deaths from disaster in 2011.

Top 5 natural disasters by number of deaths

Countries	Event in 2011	By number of deaths
Japan	Earthquake/ Tsunami	19,847
Philippines	Tropical cyclone 'Washi'	1,439
Brazil	Flood	900
Thailand	Flood	813
Turkey	Earthquake	604

Top 5 countries affected by natural disasters in 2011, by different categories

By deaths per 100,000 of the population

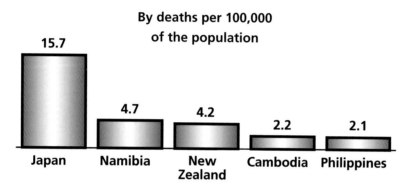

Japan	Namibia	New Zealand	Cambodia	Philippines
15.7	4.7	4.2	2.2	2.1

By number of victims (millions)

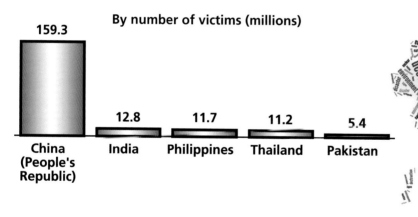

China (People's Republic)	India	Philippines	Thailand	Pakistan
159.3	12.8	11.7	11.2	5.4

By victims as % of population

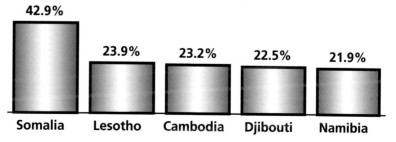

Somalia	Lesotho	Cambodia	Djibouti	Namibia
42.9%	23.9%	23.2%	22.5%	21.9%

Source: Annual Disaster Statistical Review 2011 – The numbers and trends, Centre for Research on the Epidemiology of Disasters - CRED; International Federation of Red Cross and Red Crescent Societies
www.cred.be
www.ifrc.org/

SEE ALSO:
www.completeissues.co.uk

Spilled and spoiled

Food waste deprives hungry people and damages the environment

One person in every **seven** in the world is going **hungry**

One third of food produced for human consumption **is wasted**

How this affects the environment

Nearly **a third of greenhouse gases** are linked to **agriculture** through:

- food production;
- cutting down forests for farming land;
- transport;
- landfill.

These contribute to climate change and the negative effects make it difficult for farmers to supply the world with food.

In **developing countries** food losses happen from harvest to market.

In **high income countries**, most of the waste occurs after the food reaches the consumer.

What causes the waste?

In many **developing countries**, most food is produced by small-scale farmers who are already facing up to extreme weather and a changing climate. They have difficulties in harvesting the food, getting it to market and getting a fair price.

From soil to shop

- Poor timing and methods of harvesting;
- Attacks on crops by birds, rodents and insects;
- Spoilage in transit;
- Lack of transport systems to get crops to market;
- Losses in storage and processing;
- Crops discarded as not up to standard;
- Damage from inappropriate packaging;
- Poor shop storage – especially where no cold storage is available.

In developed countries, shops and food outlets have enough food available to provide each and every person with more than 3,000 calories per day. On average, an adult only needs to eat around 2,000 calories each day. These extra calories contribute to the obesity problem or end up in our bins as wasted food which often goes to landfill sites producing greenhouse gases.

Where we waste food

- Confusion about best before/use by dates – food is thrown away;
- Wasteful preparation – usable parts are thrown away;
- Poor storage;
- Excess buying;
- Significant amounts are left on the plate;
- Food waste which could be separated out for animal feed goes into landfill.

Food waste per head, kg per year

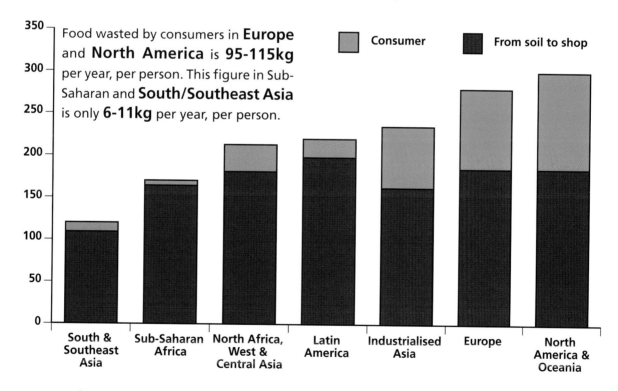

Food wasted by consumers in **Europe** and **North America** is **95-115kg** per year, per person. This figure in Sub-Saharan and **South/Southeast Asia** is only **6-11kg** per year, per person.

Legend: Consumer / From soil to shop

Categories: South & Southeast Asia; Sub-Saharan Africa; North Africa, West & Central Asia; Latin America; Industrialised Asia; Europe; North America & Oceania

Food waste by consumers in industrialised countries amounts to **222 million tonnes** – almost as much as total food production in sub-Saharan Africa – **230 million tonnes**

Source: The Food Transformation, Oxfam; Global Food losses and food waste, UN Food and Agriculture Organization
www.oxfam.org.uk
www.fao.org/ag/ags

SEE ALSO:
www.completeissues.co.uk

Stand by for a surge

29% of CO2 emissions in the UK come from our homes and our desire for gizmos and gadgets is likely to increase this

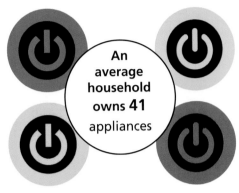

An average household owns **41** appliances

CO2 emissions make a big contribution to global warming.

Many domestic devices have become much more energy efficient – but the way we use them cancels this out.

Electricity used by devices on standby or using energy when not actually doing their job, is between **9%** and **16**% of the electricity we use in our homes.

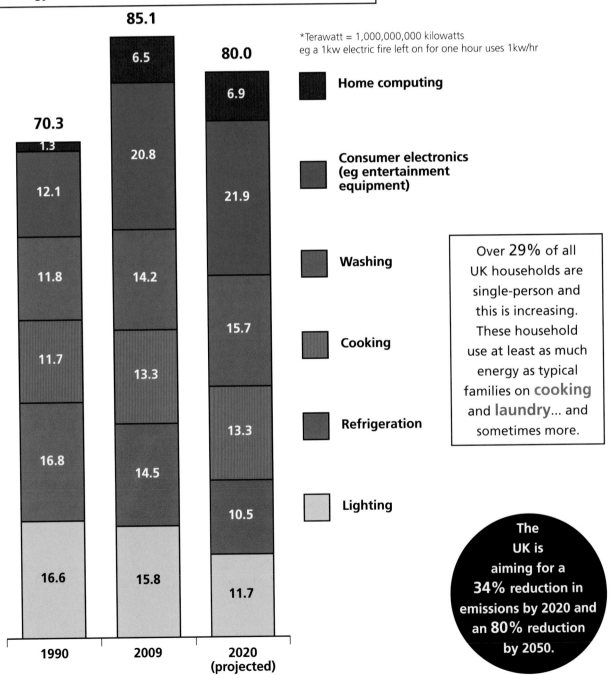

Energy use for domestic products in Terawatt* hours (TWh)

*Terawatt = 1,000,000,000 kilowatts
eg a 1kw electric fire left on for one hour uses 1kw/hr

85.1
6.5
20.8
14.2
13.3
14.5
15.8

70.3
1.3
12.1
11.8
11.7
16.8
16.6

80.0
6.9
21.9
15.7
13.3
10.5
11.7

- ■ Home computing
- ■ Consumer electronics (eg entertainment equipment)
- ■ Washing
- ■ Cooking
- ■ Refrigeration
- ■ Lighting

1990   2009   2020 (projected)

Over **29%** of all UK households are single-person and this is increasing. These household use at least as much energy as typical families on **cooking** and **laundry**... and sometimes more.

The UK is aiming for a **34%** reduction in emissions by 2020 and an **80%** reduction by 2050.

Devices are much more efficient now

for example fridges use **50%** less electricity than 15 years ago **but...**

Home computing – More portable devices means more chargers plugged in all the time. Routine tasks, such as reading and shopping, now done on gadgets, will mean more demand.

Distribution of energy use in 2009 and 2020 (projected)

Success! We have cut energy use on lighting thanks to low energy lightbulbs. 300 million of them have been given away or subsidised since 2008.

Refrigeration – Larger, American-style fridge-freezers and new features such as ice makers and water chillers will consume more energy.

Consumer electronics – We use our home entertainment equipment more than was thought – we watch about six hours a day of television, not five. That's an extra **400 hours** of viewing per household.

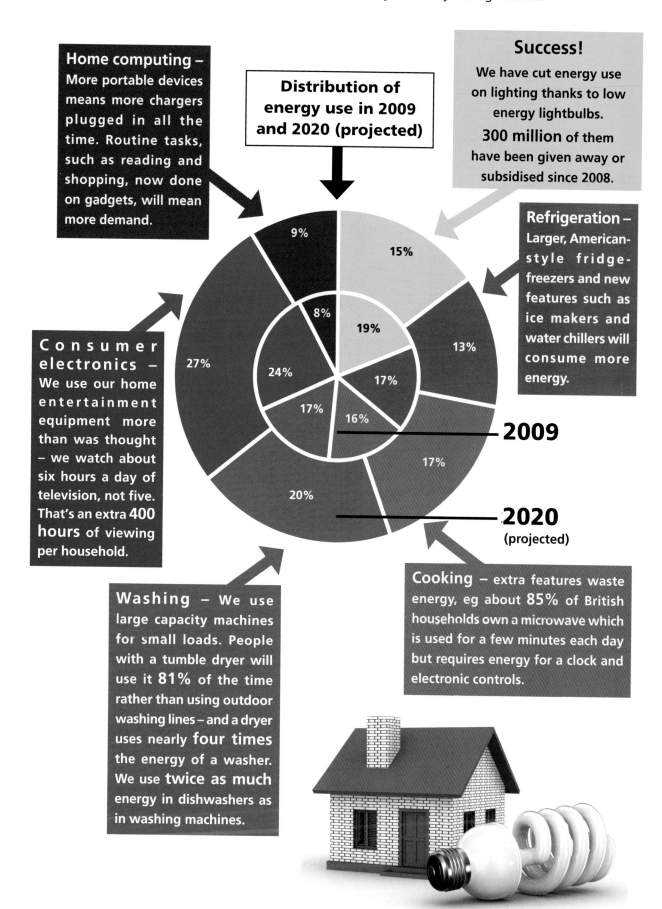

2009

2020 (projected)

Washing – We use large capacity machines for small loads. People with a tumble dryer will use it **81%** of the time rather than using outdoor washing lines – and a dryer uses nearly **four times** the energy of a washer. We use **twice as much** energy in dishwashers as in washing machines.

Cooking – extra features waste energy, eg about **85%** of British households own a microwave which is used for a few minutes each day but requires energy for a clock and electronic controls.

Pie chart values: 9%, 15%, 8%, 19%, 13%, 27%, 24%, 17%, 17%, 16%, 20%, 17%

Source: The Elephant in the Living Room, 2011 & Powering the Nation, 2012, Energy Saving Trust
www.energysavingtrust.org.uk

SEE ALSO: www.completeissues.co.uk

Down the drain

70% of the Earth is covered with water but only about 1% of that is readily available for human use...
...why are we wasting it?

 97% of the earth's water is salty or otherwise undrinkable. 2% is locked in the ice caps and glaciers

 That leaves just 1% for all humanity's needs.

If you could pour all of the world's water into a 4 litre jug, only one tablespoon of it would be available for us to use.

Since life began, we have had the same amount of water on the planet. Life can only exist with water.

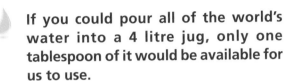

Where does the most household water wastage occur?

The toilet accounts for 63% of the water we use at home.

Flushing a used tissue or cotton bud can waste about 7 litres per time.

Leaking taps waste at least 5,500 litres of water a year: that's enough water wasted to fill a paddling pool every week for the whole summer.

Our critical water situation is due to a combination of:

Increased demand
We are all using more per person than 10 years ago and on average demand has grown by 1% a year since 1930.

 +

Increased population

+

Changes in rainfall patterns
An increase in rainfall intensity makes it difficult to store.

Although household water wastage is a problem, a huge amount of water is being lost before it even reaches the tap

Of the 14,770 megalitres supplied in England & Wales in 2010/11, 22% was lost through leakage

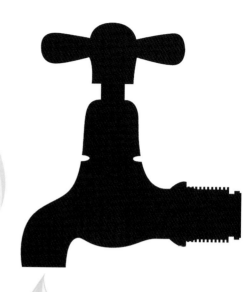

Megalitres of water lost per day and % of daily supply, England and Wales

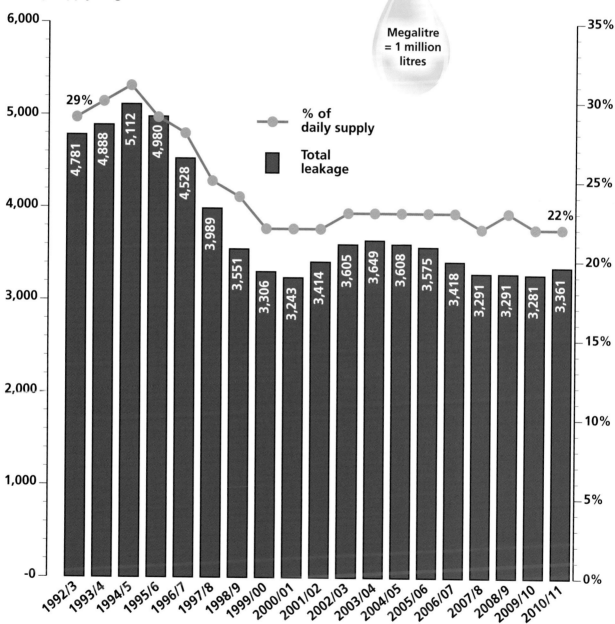

Megalitre = 1 million litres

- ● % of daily supply
- ■ Total leakage

29%

22%

Year	Total leakage
1992/3	4,781
1993/4	4,888
1994/5	5,112
1995/6	4,980
1996/7	4,528
1997/8	3,989
1998/9	3,551
1999/00	3,306
2000/01	3,243
2001/02	3,414
2002/03	3,605
2003/04	3,649
2004/05	3,608
2005/06	3,575
2006/07	3,418
2007/8	3,291
2008/9	3,291
2009/10	3,281
2010/11	3,361

Source: Waterwise; Ofwat; Defra – Department for Environment, Food and Rural Affairs © Crown copyright 2012
www.waterwise.org.uk
www.ofwat.gov.uk
www.defra.gov.uk

SEE ALSO:
www.completeissues.co.uk

Green spaces

92% of people think it's important to have public gardens and parks, yet only 56% use them at least once a week

21% of people reported using green spaces less than once a month or never

People were asked for the three most important reasons for spending time in public gardens, parks, commons or other green spaces:

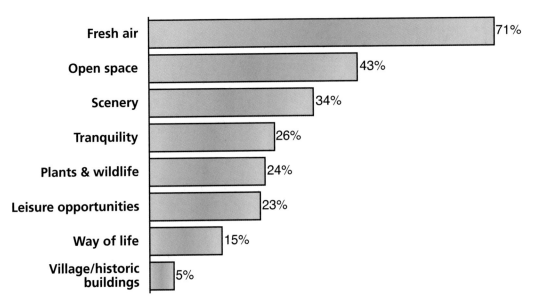

Fresh air	71%
Open space	43%
Scenery	34%
Tranquility	26%
Plants & wildlife	24%
Leisure opportunities	23%
Way of life	15%
Village/historic buildings	5%

Note: ecosystem services are the processes by which the environment produces resources such as clean air, water, food and materials

Total percentage of people who had heard of the following environmental issues:

- Climate change — 88%
- Ecosystem services — 51%
- Biodiversity — 48%

People were asked how much they agreed with the following statements:

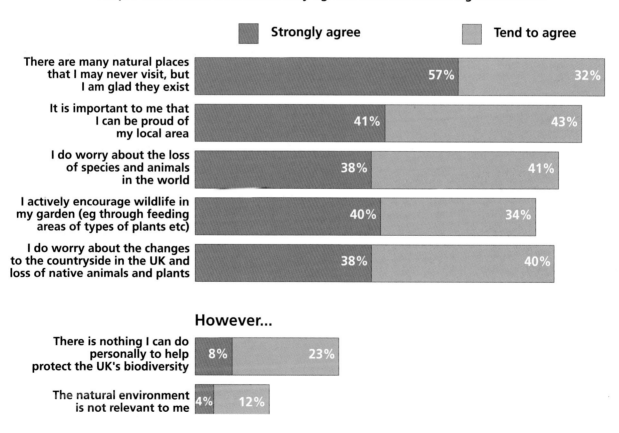

Strongly agree　　Tend to agree

There are many natural places that I may never visit, but I am glad they exist — 57% / 32%

It is important to me that I can be proud of my local area — 41% / 43%

I do worry about the loss of species and animals in the world — 38% / 41%

I actively encourage wildlife in my garden (eg through feeding areas of types of plants etc) — 40% / 34%

I do worry about the changes to the countryside in the UK and loss of native animals and plants — 38% / 40%

However...

There is nothing I can do personally to help protect the UK's biodiversity — 8% / 23%

The natural environment is not relevant to me — 4% / 12%

Base: 1,769 adults in England

Sources: Attitudes and knowledge relating to biodiversity and the natural environment, 2007 - 2011, Defra © Crown copyright, CAPI omnibus tns www.defra.gov.uk

SEE ALSO:
www.completeissues.co.uk

Wasting away

We are managing to dispose of waste in a more environmentally friendly way

Disposing of the waste we generate is a problem. Landfill sites (rubbish dumps) are ugly and have to be carefully managed to avoid toxic water or gases leaking into the environment. The soil can remain contaminated even after a site is no longer used.

Incinerators can also release chemicals into the atmosphere which may have dangers for health. Neither landfill nor incineration plants are popular with communities living near them.

Recycling or composting seems to offer a better alternative.

Methods of Waste Disposal, UK*

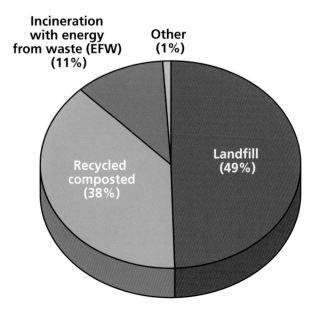

Incineration with energy from waste (EFW) (11%)
Other (1%)
Recycled composted (38%)
Landfill (49%)

Household Waste Disposal, kg per household per year, England, 2010/11

■ Waste recycled/ composted/reused

■ Waste NOT recycled/ composted/reused

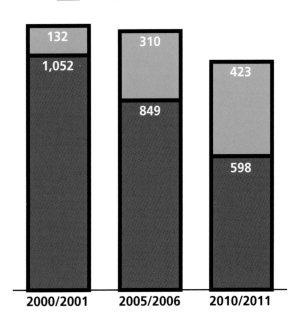

	2000/2001	2005/2006	2010/2011
Recycled	132	310	423
Not recycled	1,052	849	598

In 2011 in England each person created
445 kg of household waste.

Less than half of this,
191 kg was **recycled**.

*Data for UK is 2009/10 as it is collected later than data for individual countries

Source: Defra © Crown copyright 2012
www.defra.gov.uk

SEE ALSO:
www.completeissues.co.uk

Family & relationships

Family figures

Although the nature of the family is gradually changing, married couples are still the most common family type

What is a household?

A **household** is not the same as a **family**. It can be one person living alone, or a group of people living at the same address, sharing cooking and living facilities.

What is a family?

A **family** is a married, civil partnered or cohabiting couple with or without children, or a lone parent with at least one child.

A **household** can consist of **more than one family** or **no families**.

Most **households** consist of one **family** – a couple with or without children.

Households: by household type, UK
(millions)

2001

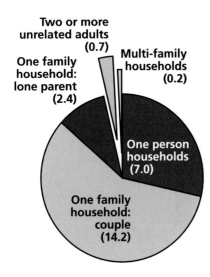

Two or more unrelated adults (0.7)

Multi-family households (0.2)

One family household: lone parent (2.4)

One person households (7.0)

One family household: couple (14.2)

24.5m households

2011

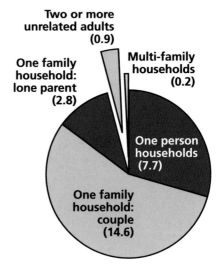

Two or more unrelated adults (0.9)

Multi-family households (0.2)

One family household: lone parent (2.8)

One person households (7.7)

One family household: couple (14.6)

26.3m households

Family types

Opposite sex couples

12 million married couples (down **262,000** on 2001)

2.9 million cohabiting couples (up from **2.1 million** in 2001)

Same sex couples

63,000 families cohabiting, 59,000 civil partnered

Lone parents

2 million with **dependent children** **92%** of these parents are women. They form **26%** of all families with dependent children

Families: by family type
(thousands)

There were **17.9 million families** in the UK in 2011.

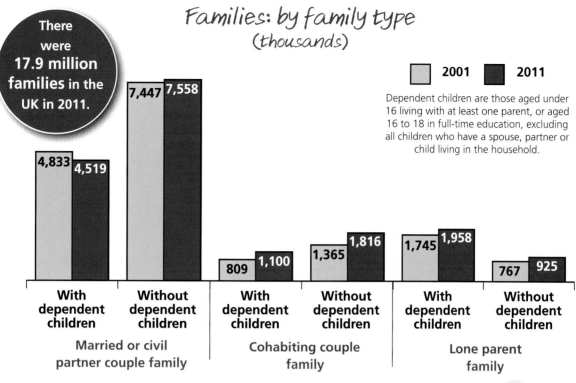

	2001	2011

Dependent children are those aged under 16 living with at least one parent, or aged 16 to 18 in full-time education, excluding all children who have a spouse, partner or child living in the household.

7,447 | **7,558**

4,833 | **4,519**

809 | **1,100**

1,365 | **1,816**

1,745 | **1,958**

767 | **925**

With dependent children	Without dependent children	With dependent children	Without dependent children	With dependent children	Without dependent children
Married or civil partner couple family		Cohabiting couple family		Lone parent family	

Percentage of families, by number of dependent children in the family

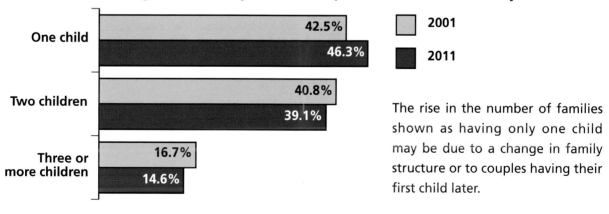

	2001	2011

One child — 42.5% / 46.3%

Two children — 40.8% / 39.1%

Three or more children — 16.7% / 14.6%

The rise in the number of families shown as having only one child may be due to a change in family structure or to couples having their first child later.

Source: Statistical Bulletin, Families and Households 2001 to 2011, published 2012 © Crown copyright 2012
www.ons.gov.uk

Just listen

Regardless of family structure, young people appreciate being valued

After interviewing more than 30,000 children aged eight to 16,
The Good Childhood Report reveals what affects a young person's sense of well-being.
Young people were asked score ten important aspects of their lives,
where zero meant 'very unhappy' and 10 meant 'very happy'.

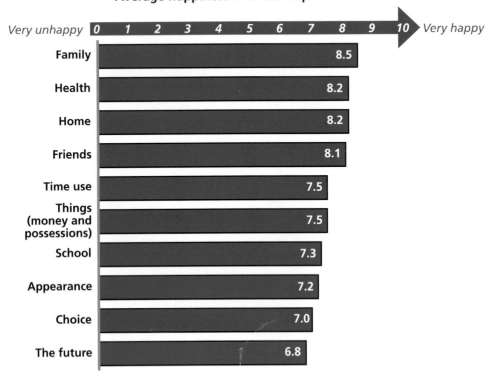

Average happiness with ten aspects of life

Very unhappy 0 1 2 3 4 5 6 7 8 9 10 Very happy

Family	8.5
Health	8.2
Home	8.2
Friends	8.1
Time use	7.5
Things (money and possessions)	7.5
School	7.3
Appearance	7.2
Choice	7.0
The future	6.8

Children's relationships with family and other carers are extremely important to their well-being. Families come in a wide variety of forms in the UK today. It is becoming increasingly difficult to categorise family structures.

For example, 17% of children aged 10 to 15 said that they lived in more than one home. How much does this affect well-being?

Safety, security and stability within the family were recurring themes in children's comments:

'Having a good, safe home with loving parents.'

'A stable family with parents or carers who love and provide for you.'

At the same time, children also identified the importance of being listened to:

'They should listen to the child.'

Family structure is not crucial to well-being – it is relationships that matter. Almost identical numbers of those interviewed said their families did or did not get on well whether the family had both parents, step parents or a lone parent.

Percentage of young people who felt they were listened to and helped make family decisions

■ My parents or carers listen to my views and take me seriously

■ I help make decisions in my family

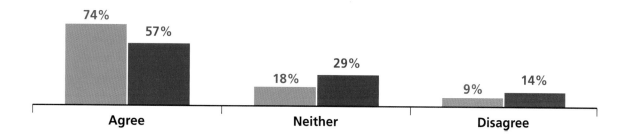

	Agree	Neither	Disagree
My parents or carers listen	74%	18%	9%
I help make decisions	57%	29%	14%

There was a difference depending on age and gender.

Year 10 children (aged 14 to 15) were more likely to feel they weren't being listened to and taken seriously than Year 8 children (aged 12 to 13). This suggests that there is perhaps an increasing mismatch between parents' treatment and children's own expectations as they grow older.

10% of girls felt they weren't being listened to and taken seriously compared to 7% of boys. There was no gender difference in relation to the question about involvement in family decision-making.

'A happy family is a family which communicates and supports each other. Loving each other, supporting, but allowing teenagers to grow up.'

Source: Good Childhood Report 2012, The Children's Society
www.childrenssociety.org.uk

SEE ALSO:
www.completeissues.co.uk

Taking more care?

The number of children in the care of local authorities in England has increased. Does this mean the system is working better?

Each year a 'snapshot' is taken of the numbers of children in care on 31st March

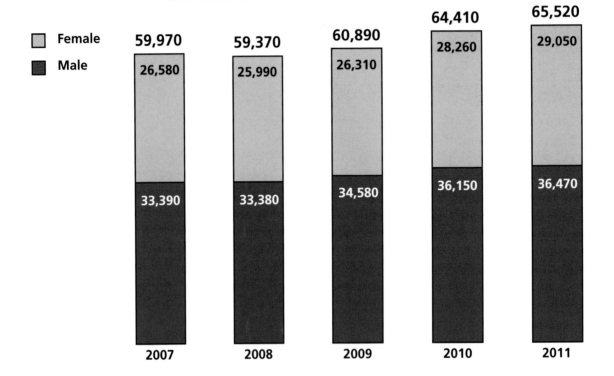

□ Female
■ Male

	2007	2008	2009	2010	2011
Total	59,970	59,370	60,890	64,410	65,520
Female	26,580	25,990	26,310	28,260	29,050
Male	33,390	33,380	34,580	36,150	36,470

Reason for being looked after at 31 March 2011

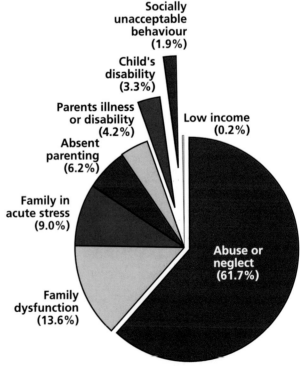

Socially unacceptable behaviour (1.9%)

Child's disability (3.3%)

Parents illness or disability (4.2%)

Low income (0.2%)

Absent parenting (6.2%)

Family in acute stress (9.0%)

Abuse or neglect (61.7%)

Family dysfunction (13.6%)

In order to take over the care of a child, a local authority must go to court and gain a care order. It must show that a child Is not receiving the sort of care it would be reasonable to expect from a parent and that this is causing the child significant harm.

Cafcass – The Children and Family Court Advisory and Support Service – exists to support the welfare of children involved in those proceedings. It has noted a rise of **62%** in the number of care applications between 2007/8 and 2011/12.

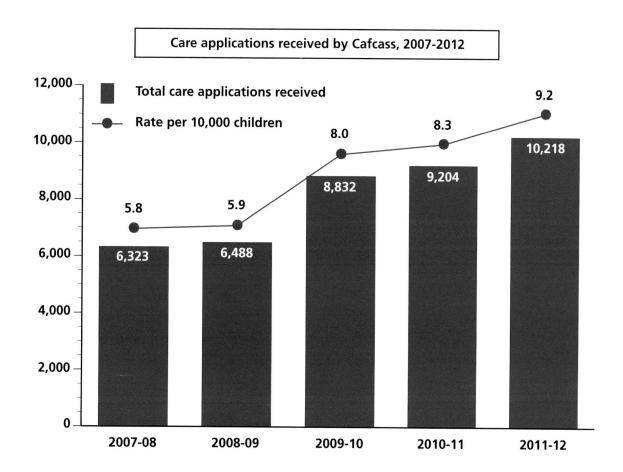

Care applications received by Cafcass, 2007-2012

- Total care applications received
- Rate per 10,000 children

Year	Total care applications received	Rate per 10,000 children
2007-08	6,323	5.8
2008-09	6,488	5.9
2009-10	8,832	8.0
2010-11	9,204	8.3
2011-12	10,218	9.2

The 'Baby Peter Effect'

Peter Connelly, aged 17 months, died on 3rd August 2007 after months of cruelty and neglect at the hands of his mother, her boyfriend and his brother.

Several agencies had registered concern and had contact with the family but no one acted in time to save the child.

It appears that the case, which came to court in 2009, changed attitudes and made authorities more likely to intervene. This effect is still being seen three years on.

Source: Department for Education, Children Looked After by Local Authorities in England;
Three weeks in November ... three years on,
Cafcass care application study 2012 © Crown copyright
www.education.gov.uk/adoptionscorecards
www.cafcass.gov.uk/news/2012/cafcass_care_study_2012.aspx

SEE ALSO:
Baby P's legacy, p70, Fact File 2010
The lessons that need to be learnt from Baby P, p94, Essential Articles 12
www.completeissues.co.uk

Believe in children

Adults hold a negative view of all children...

...even though the majority are well behaved, attend school, take part in activities and many volunteer and contribute to their communities

A representative sample of **2,102** UK adults were asked whether they agreed or **disagreed** with each of the following statements that had been made about young people in the UK:

Children in this country are becoming feral

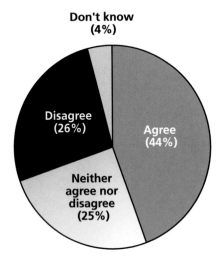

Don't know (4%)
Disagree (26%)
Agree (44%)
Neither agree nor disagree (25%)

British children are beginning to behave like animals

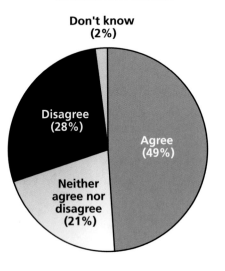

Don't know (2%)
Disagree (28%)
Agree (49%)
Neither agree nor disagree (21%)

The trouble with youngsters is that they're angry, violent and abusive

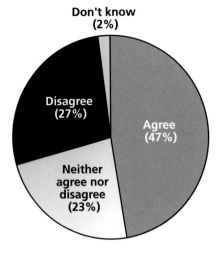

Don't know (2%)
Disagree (27%)
Agree (47%)
Neither agree nor disagree (23%)

Children who get into trouble are often misunderstood and in need of professional help

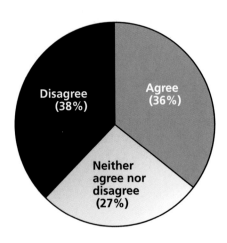

Disagree (38%)
Agree (36%)
Neither agree nor disagree (27%)

" What hope is there for childhood in the UK today if this is how adults think?...

We are unquestionably accepting a stereotype of young people as criminal and revolting **"**

Anne Marie Carrie – Chief Executive, Barnado's

NB totals may not add up to 100% due to rounding

When you think about children who behave badly or in an inappropriate/ disruptive or anti-social way – at what age do you think it is TOO LATE to help change them for the better?

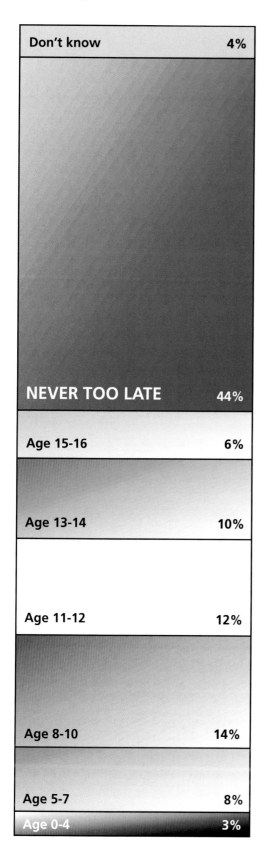

Don't know	4%
NEVER TOO LATE	44%
Age 15-16	6%
Age 13-14	10%
Age 11-12	12%
Age 8-10	14%
Age 5-7	8%
Age 0-4	3%

" We aren't asking people to put up with yobbish behaviour, but we do need to change our attitudes towards troubled children. The small minority of children who come across as angry and abusive have sadly often been scarred by their upbringing.

But it's NEVER TOO LATE to believe in children and change their life story – it doesn't have to end how it began "

Anne Marie Carrie
Chief Executive, Barnado's

Source: ICM Research on behalf of Barnado's
www.barnados.org.uk
www.icmresearch.com

SEE ALSO:
www.completeissues.co.uk

What's your name?

Trends in baby names

Most popular names for boys

	2008	2009	2010	2011
1	Jack	Oliver	Oliver	**Harry**
2	Oliver	Jack	Jack	Oliver
3	Thomas	**Harry**	**Harry**	Jack
4	**Harry**	Alfie	Alfie	Alfie
5	Joshua	Joshua	Charlie	Charlie
6	Alfie	Thomas	Thomas	Thomas
7	Charlie	Charlie	William	Jacob
8	Daniel	William	Joshua	James
9	James	James	George	Joshua
10	William	Daniel	James	William

Most popular names for girls

	2008	2009	2010	2011
1	Olivia	Olivia	Olivia	**Amelia**
2	Ruby	Ruby	Sophie	Olivia
3	Emily	Chloe	Emily	Lily
4	Grace	Emily	Lily	Jessica
5	Jessica	Sophie	**Amelia**	Emily
6	Chloe	Jessica	Jessica	Sophie
7	Sophie	Grace	Ruby	Ruby
8	Lily	Lily	Chloe	Grace
9	**Amelia**	**Amelia**	Grace	Ava
10	Evie	Evie	Evie	Isabella

Source: Office for National Statistics © Crown copyright 2012
www.ons.gov.uk

SEE ALSO:
www.completeissues.co.uk

Financial issues

Missing out

Children suffer when they are deprived of experiences and possessions that others see as normal

The Children's Society used group discussions with young people to produce a list of 10 items and experiences they considered important for *a normal kind of life*.

This was included in a survey of 5,500 young people aged 8-15 across England.

| Don't have but would like | Don't have and don't want | Have |

The 10 items or experiences were:

Some pocket money each week to spend on yourself

| 22% | 15% | 63% |

Some money that you can save each month, either in a bank or at home

| 18% | 8% | 74% |

Family trips or days out at least once a month

| 18% | 7% | 75% |

An iPod or other personal music player

| 17% | 7% | 76% |

At least one family holiday away from home each year

| 15% | 4% | 81% |

Pair of designer or brand name trainers (like Nike or Vans)

| 13% | 19% | 68% |

A garden at home, or somewhere nearby like a park where you can safely spend time with your friends

| 9% | 3% | 88% |

A family car for transport when you need it

| 7% | 3% | 90% |

The right kind of clothes to fit in with other people your age

| 6% | 3% | 91% |

Cable or satellite TV at home

| 5% | 3% | 92% |

Fact File 2013 • www.carelpress.com

Importance of the 10 items

By gender

Boys		Girls	
Item	**Rank**	**Item**	**Rank**
Clothes	1	Clothes	1
Garden	=2	TV	=2
Car	=2	Garden	=2
TV	=4	Holiday	=2
Holiday	=4	Car	=5
Trainers	6	Daytrips	=5
Daytrips	=7	iPod	=7
Pocket money	=7	Pocket money	=7
Saving	=7	Trainers	=9
iPod	=7	Saving	=9

By ethnicity

White		Non-white	
Item	**Rank**	**Item**	**Rank**
Clothes	1	Saving	=1
Garden	=2	TV	=1
Car	=2	Garden	=1
Holiday	=2	Car	=1
Daytrips	5	Clothes	=1
Saving	=6	Holiday	=6
iPod	=6	Daytrips	=6
TV	=6	Trainers	8
Trainers	9	Pocket money	=9
Pocket money	10	iPod	=9

Where children were missing out on an item from the index, they were considerably more likely to be unhappy than children who had that item – children who lack more than five out of 10 items are over five times more likely to have low levels of wellbeing than those who lack none.

Although all the items had some effect on a child's wellbeing, the right kind of clothes, a garden or park nearby, monthly day trips and cable/satellite TV had the most obvious link.

Source: Missing Out © The Children's Society
www.childrenssociety.org.uk

SEE ALSO:
www.completeissues.co.uk

Feeling the squeeze

Parents are finding it hard to cope with financial pressures

A survey of 1,924 parents by Netmums showed that
over half felt like they were **living on the edge** – a slight
rise in the cost of living or decline in their income was likely
to send them over it, **into crisis**

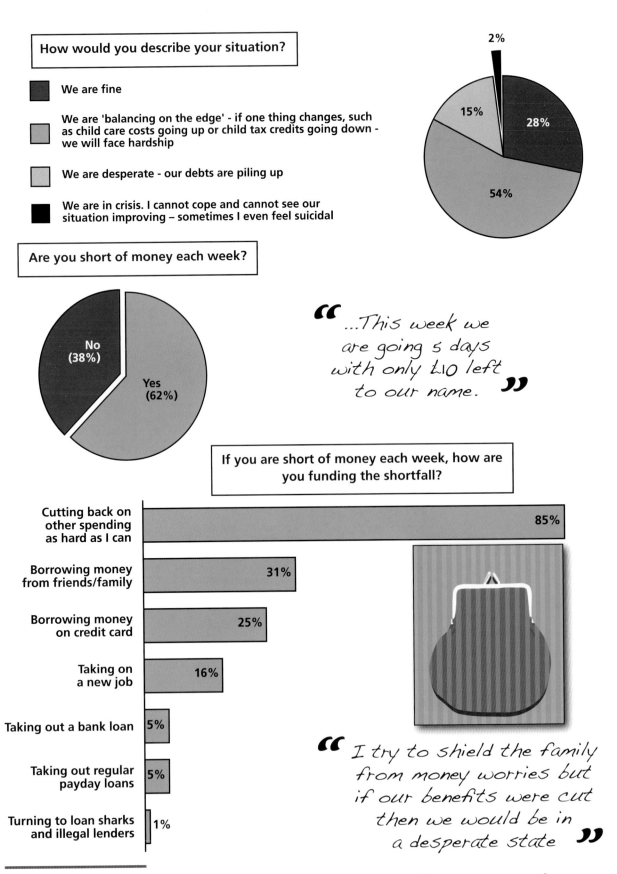

How would you describe your situation?

- **We are fine**
- **We are 'balancing on the edge'** - if one thing changes, such as child care costs going up or child tax credits going down - we will face hardship
- **We are desperate** - our debts are piling up
- **We are in crisis.** I cannot cope and cannot see our situation improving – sometimes I even feel suicidal

2%

15%

28%

54%

Are you short of money each week?

No (38%)

Yes (62%)

" ...This week we are going 5 days with only £10 left to our name. "

If you are short of money each week, how are you funding the shortfall?

Cutting back on other spending as hard as I can	85%
Borrowing money from friends/family	31%
Borrowing money on credit card	25%
Taking on a new job	16%
Taking out a bank loan	5%
Taking out regular payday loans	5%
Turning to loan sharks and illegal lenders	1%

" I try to shield the family from money worries but if our benefits were cut then we would be in a desperate state "

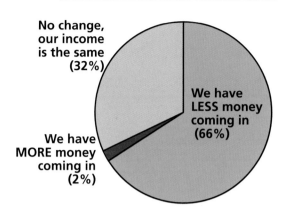

How is the current economic downturn hitting your income?

No change, our income is the same (32%)

We have LESS money coming in (66%)

We have MORE money coming in (2%)

The impact on families

While **72%** claim to be 'coping', **19%** of parents have been treated for stress or are suffering from a stress-related illness due to lack of cash, **8%** have been put on anti-depressants and **1%** have been referred for counselling to help them deal with financial pressures.

35% said their relationships with their partner had become strained through money worries.

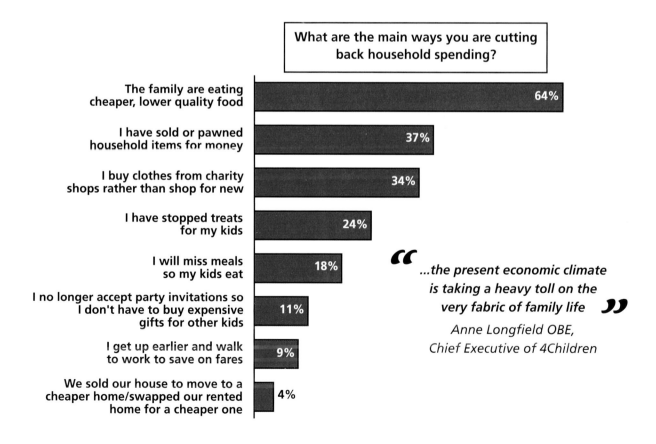

What are the main ways you are cutting back household spending?

Category	Percentage
The family are eating cheaper, lower quality food	64%
I have sold or pawned household items for money	37%
I buy clothes from charity shops rather than shop for new	34%
I have stopped treats for my kids	24%
I will miss meals so my kids eat	18%
I no longer accept party invitations so I don't have to buy expensive gifts for other kids	11%
I get up earlier and walk to work to save on fares	9%
We sold our house to move to a cheaper home/swapped our rented home for a cheaper one	4%

" *...the present economic climate is taking a heavy toll on the very fabric of family life* **"**

Anne Longfield OBE, Chief Executive of 4Children

Source: Netmums survey, February 2012
www.netmums.com

SEE ALSO:
www.completeissues.co.uk

Making ends meet

Young people don't have enough money put aside for a 'rainy day' let alone to prepare for the future

A survey looked at the saving behaviour and attitudes of 1,504 young people aged 16-29 with an income below £21,000 (the median income for this group)

Assuming you need to save for a deposit on a house, save for your pension, and to pay for care in old age, HOW MUCH savings would you need at the age of 30?

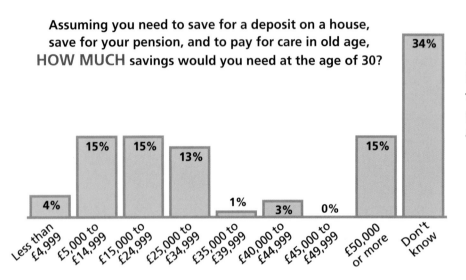

Less than £4,999	£5,000 to £14,999	£15,000 to £24,999	£25,000 to £34,999	£35,000 to £39,999	£40,000 to £44,999	£45,000 to £49,999	£50,000 or more	Don't know
4%	15%	15%	13%	1%	3%	0%	15%	34%

In fact, around **£25,000** is needed for a deposit to buy a house, before pension and other costs are taken into account.

If you became unexpectedly unemployed, HOW LONG could you 'make ends meet'?

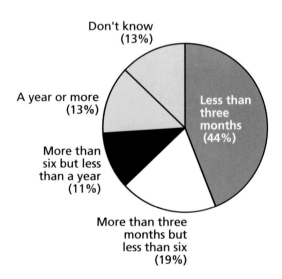

- Don't know (13%)
- A year or more (13%)
- More than six but less than a year (11%)
- More than three months but less than six (19%)
- Less than three months (44%)

17% of low earning young people felt they would last **less than one month**

NB Totals may not add up to 100% due to rounding

HOW would you 'make ends meet' if you became suddenly unemployed

(More than one answer could be given)

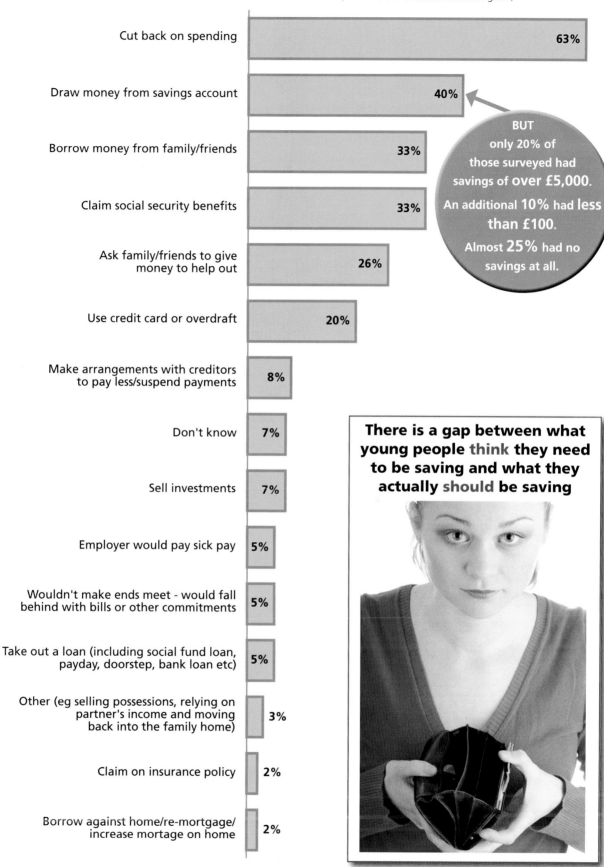

Response	%
Cut back on spending	63%
Draw money from savings account	40%
Borrow money from family/friends	33%
Claim social security benefits	33%
Ask family/friends to give money to help out	26%
Use credit card or overdraft	20%
Make arrangements with creditors to pay less/suspend payments	8%
Don't know	7%
Sell investments	7%
Employer would pay sick pay	5%
Wouldn't make ends meet - would fall behind with bills or other commitments	5%
Take out a loan (including social fund loan, payday, doorstep, bank loan etc)	5%
Other (eg selling possessions, relying on partner's income and moving back into the family home)	3%
Claim on insurance policy	2%
Borrow against home/re-mortgage/ increase mortage on home	2%

BUT only 20% of those surveyed had savings of **over £5,000**.

An additional **10%** had **less than £100**.

Almost **25%** had no savings at all.

There is a gap between what young people think they need to be saving and what they actually should be saving

Source: Young People and savings – YouGov on behalf of Institute for Public Policy Research (IPPR), February 2012
www.ippr.org
http://research.yougov.co.uk

SEE ALSO:
www.completeissues.co.uk

Loaded loans

Are payday loans easing the burden of debt or increasing it?

A payday loan is a small, short-term loan usually used to cover expenses until the next payday

Last year the payday loan sector in Britain was worth **£1.7bn**, a fivefold increase in the last few years. Research predicts nearly **4 million** people will take out a payday loan in the next six months alone.

£ £ £ £ £

The interest charged for payday lenders can begin at **444%** and can escalate to **16,500%** or more. Home credit lenders, who make home visits in order to collect repayments for their short-term loans, can charge **£82** in interest and collection charges for every **£100** lent.

£ £ £ £ £

98% of MPs and **93%** of the public believe there is a problem with payday lending

Q: People were asked:
Which of the following changes, if any, do you think should be made in order to protect consumers from short-term, high interest payday loan lending?

Stricter regulation of advertising, with clear warnings about the true cost of total debt
 68%

A limit on the total cost that can be charged for credit
 65%

A limit on the number of loans, to ensure that the original loan and interest has been paid off before a new loan is taken out
 48%

A central register to prevent people taking out multiple loans with different lenders
 46%

None, I do not think there is a problem
 7%

Those who thought there should be stricter restriction on the advertising of payday loans, by age

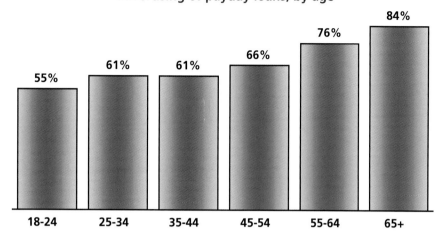

18-24	25-34	35-44	45-54	55-64	65+
55%	61%	61%	66%	76%	84%

£££££ Research published by Which? showed **61%** of payday loan users had used the money for essentials – paying bills and buying household essentials like food.

£££££ One payday loan firm posted a pre-tax profit of **£162m** last year, and another paid its chief executive **£1.6m**.

Base: 2,044 GB adults

Source: Payday loan survey, Comres, 2012
www.comres.co.uk

SEE ALSO:
Quids in, Essential Articles 15, p73
www.completeissues.co.uk

Unaffordable

The gap between earnings and house prices puts buying a home out of reach of many people

2001

Average house price, England:	£121,769
Average salary:	£16,557
The ratio between average house price and salary:	7.4

2011

Average house price, England: – an increase of **94%** since 2001	£236,518
Average salary: – an increase of **29%** since 2001	£21,330
The ratio between average house price and salary:	11.1

Overall % increase in ratio 2001 to 2011 **51%**

Unaffordable 2011

Areas of England where the gap between average house prices and wages has increased most between 2001 and 2011

% increase in ratio 2001 to 2011

- 2011 house prices
- 2011 median earnings

132% Copeland, Cumbria — £129,862 / £21,117

103% Watford, Herfordshire — £246,455 / £15,272

100% Corby, Northamptonshire — £132,381 / £18,522

99% Redcar & Cleveland — £122,936 / £16,968

91% Burnley, Lancashire — £89,240 / £17,540

In 2001 the deposit for a typical **90% mortgage** was **£12,177** – about 9 months salary.

In **2011** the amount banks were willing to lend was less, and so the deposit needed for a typical **75% mortgage** was **£59,129**, almost **three years** salary.

Source: National Housing Federation
www.housing.org.uk

SEE ALSO:
www.completeissues.co.uk

Food & drink

Savvy shoppers

People are taking advantage of offers, cheaper brands and planning ahead to save money on food

97% of shoppers believed the cost of their typical shopping basket had gone up significantly in the last three years.

On average, they thought their weekly shopping bill was now about £15 more expensive.

What do you do to get the most out of your food shopping?
(more than one answer could be given)

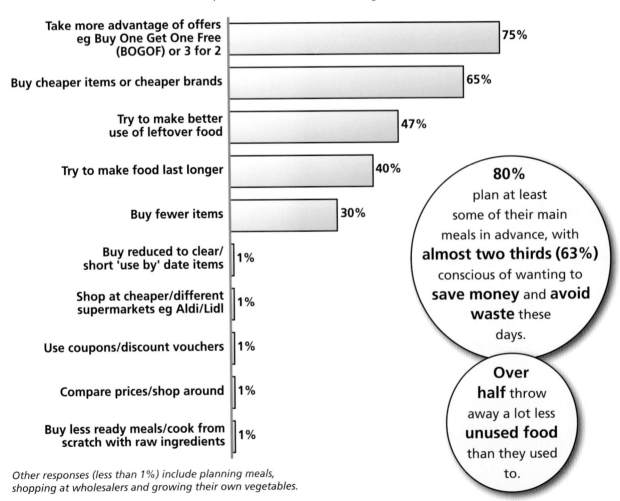

Take more advantage of offers eg Buy One Get One Free (BOGOF) or 3 for 2	75%
Buy cheaper items or cheaper brands	65%
Try to make better use of leftover food	47%
Try to make food last longer	40%
Buy fewer items	30%
Buy reduced to clear/ short 'use by' date items	1%
Shop at cheaper/different supermarkets eg Aldi/Lidl	1%
Use coupons/discount vouchers	1%
Compare prices/shop around	1%
Buy less ready meals/cook from scratch with raw ingredients	1%

80% plan at least some of their main meals in advance, with **almost two thirds (63%)** conscious of wanting to **save money** and **avoid waste** these days.

Over half throw away a lot less **unused food** than they used to.

Other responses (less than 1%) include planning meals, shopping at wholesalers and growing their own vegetables.

89% of those asked always or sometimes **check what is in their cupboards** and make a list of what they need before doing the main food shop

Shopping list

Bread
Milk
Marg
Apples
Bananas
Potatoes
Carrots
Onions
Beans
Tomatoes
Stock cubes

Tea
Coffee
Sugar

61% of those who make a shopping list sometimes stick to it. Some people **(86%)** don't stick to their list because they are tempted away by good offers, promotions and deals.

57% of people said that using leftovers was a good way to save money.

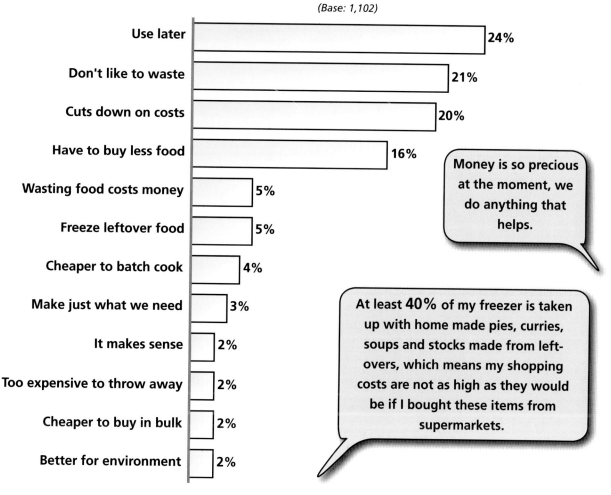

People who strongly agreed that using leftovers was a good way to save money were asked for their reasons

(Base: 1,102)

Use later	24%
Don't like to waste	21%
Cuts down on costs	20%
Have to buy less food	16%
Wasting food costs money	5%
Freeze leftover food	5%
Cheaper to batch cook	4%
Make just what we need	3%
It makes sense	2%
Too expensive to throw away	2%
Cheaper to buy in bulk	2%
Better for environment	2%

Money is so precious at the moment, we do anything that helps.

At least **40%** of my freezer is taken up with home made pies, curries, soups and stocks made from left-overs, which means my shopping costs are not as high as they would be if I bought these items from supermarkets.

Base: Food Standards Agency online survey of 1,906 UK adults aged 18-64

Source: Food Standards Agency © Crown copyright 2012
www.food.gov.uk

SEE ALSO:
Leftovers, p88-89
www.completeissues.co.uk

Leftovers

Some people are taking more risks with food safety as they try to save money and make their meals go further

A Food Standards Agency online survey of 1,906 UK adults aged 18-64 showed that **97%** believed the cost of their typical shopping basket had gone up significantly in the last three years – **47%** of these were trying to make better use of leftover food.

What do you do with leftover food?
(Only one answer could be chosen from the following statements)

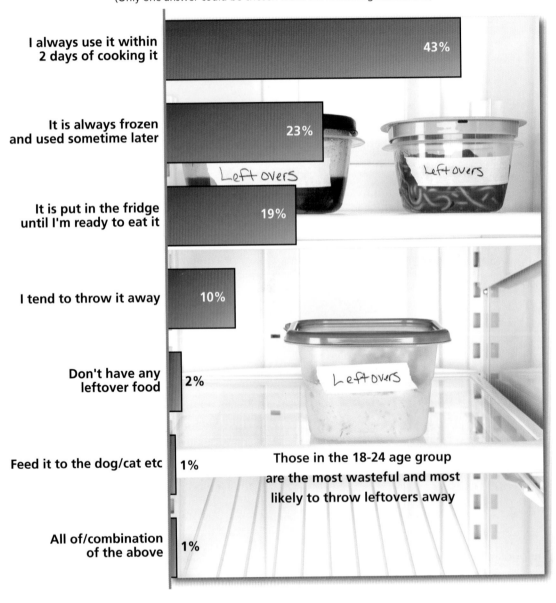

I always use it within 2 days of cooking it	43%
It is always frozen and used sometime later	23%
It is put in the fridge until I'm ready to eat it	19%
I tend to throw it away	10%
Don't have any leftover food	2%
Feed it to the dog/cat etc	1%
All of/combination of the above	1%

Those in the 18-24 age group are the most wasteful and most likely to throw leftovers away

"Using leftovers is a good way of making our meals go further. However, unless we're careful there's chance we can risk food poisoning by not storing or handling them properly.

Bob Martin, Food Safety Expert, Food Standards Agency

Attitudes towards leftover food

57% said using leftover food was a good way to save money

16% said they re-used leftover food now much more than they used to

12% said they were not sure when it was safe to eat leftover food

8% said they were concerned about re-heating leftover food

8% said they would like to re-use leftover food more

Attitudes towards use by dates

Understanding use by and best before dates

Use by dates appear on foods that go off quickly. It can be dangerous to eat food past this date, even though it might look and smell fine. If cooked or frozen its life can be extended.

Once food with a **use by** date has been opened, follow any storage instructions such as 'eat within 3 days of opening'.

Best before dates appear on food with a longer shelf life. They show how long the food will be at its best quality. Using food after the **best before** doesn't mean it will be unsafe.

31% Judge food on the smell, look and how long it has been stored

22% Don't follow use by dates as strictly as they used to

29% Always stick to use by dates

11% Think use by dates are a way supermarkets make you buy more

7% Never follow use by dates on food

Source: Food Standards Agency © Crown copyright 2012
www.food.gov.uk

SEE ALSO:
Savvy shoppers, p96-97
www.completeissues.co.uk

Lunch counter

Has the drive to improve the quality and take-up rate of school lunches succeeded?

Food choices for school lunches

Available every day:
Two portions of fruit and vegetables, drinking water, healthier drinks: low-fat milk, fruit juice, bread with no added fat or oil

Available regularly:
Oily fish - at least once every three weeks

Restricted:
Starchy food cooked in fat or oil on not more than three days a week

Deep-fried food not more than twice a week

Meat products (manufactured or homemade) from four separate groups eg burgers, sausage, meat pies, breaded or coated meats – only one product from each group per fortnight

Not allowed:
Snacks high in salt and fat eg crisps

No salt to add to food after cooking

Confectionery

Percentage take-up of secondary school lunches

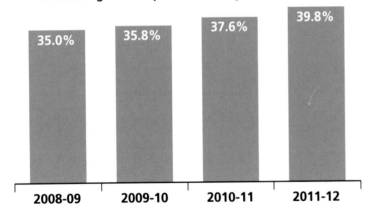

2008-09	2009-10	2010-11	2011-12
35.0%	35.8%	37.6%	39.8%

All school lunches have to meet tough standards for the type of food and nutrition offered. There are no regulations about packed lunches.

School lunches provide better nutrition than packed lunches

Pupils who eat a packed lunch do not have the same balance in what they eat.
72% of pupils who ate a **school lunch** had some fruit or vegetables as part of their meal compared with **56%** of pupils who had a **packed lunch**.

Portions of fruit and vegetables eaten, Secondary Schools, England, 2011

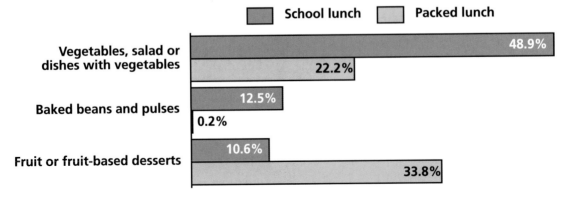

School lunch   Packed lunch

Vegetables, salad or dishes with vegetables: 48.9% / 22.2%
Baked beans and pulses: 12.5% / 0.2%
Fruit or fruit-based desserts: 10.6% / 33.8%

Nutritional standards for school lunches

School lunches should provide **30%** of daily energy requirements (kilocalories). At least **50%** of that energy should come from carbohydrates and not more than **35%** should come from fats (and only **11%** of this from saturated fats). The remaining energy requirement should come from protein.

30% of daily energy for this age group should be between **614** and **678** kilocalories. School lunches come closest to this with **25%** of daily energy compared to **23%** in packed lunches.

Main energy intake, Secondary Schools, England, 2011

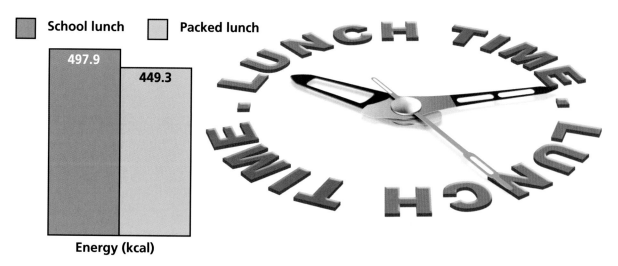

■ School lunch   □ Packed lunch

497.9
449.3

Energy (kcal)

The calories in school lunches come from better sources, with more carbohydrate and protein but less fat and less salt.

Source of main energy intake
% energy from

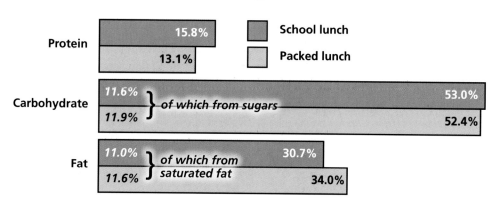

■ School lunch
□ Packed lunch

Protein — 15.8% / 13.1%

Carbohydrate — 11.6% } of which from sugars — 53.0% / 11.9% } 52.4%

Fat — 11.0% } of which from saturated fat — 30.7% / 11.6% } 34.0%

Pupils may have other reasons than nutrition for not taking up school lunches: wanting to be with friends, value for money, preferred food choices, not having to queue for food.

300,000 who are eligible for Free School Meals are not taking this up – often because of the stigma attached to it.

Base: 5,969 pupils who have school lunches
1,823 pupils who have packed lunches

Source: School Food Trust
www.schoolfoodtrust.org.uk

SEE ALSO:
www.completeissues.co.uk

Generation Y not?

Going out to eat and drink is considered a lifestyle, not a luxury, for Generation Y

Generation Y (18-34 year olds), is a loose term for people born from approximately 1982 onwards.

Generation Y are the first generation to grow up with home computers, mobile phones and multi-channel television. But in the UK they also face high unemployment and a low expectation of owning their own homes.

However, they go out **62%** more than the national average. That's up **13%** from 2011.

Generation Y is now going out **32 times a month**, which is **twice as often** as 35-54 year olds and more than **three times as often** as the over 55s.

Where people go for food and drink, visits per month:

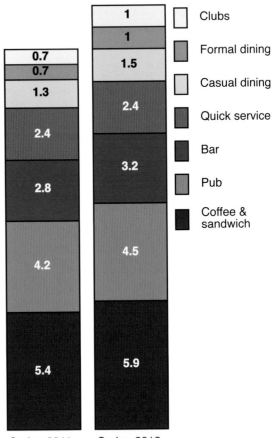

Spring 2011 | Spring 2012

Clubs
Formal dining
Casual dining
Quick service
Bar
Pub
Coffee & sandwich

Spring 2011: 0.7, 0.7, 1.3, 2.4, 2.8, 4.2, 5.4

Spring 2012: 1, 1, 1.5, 2.4, 3.2, 4.5, 5.9

24% of consumers use **social media** in search of discount vouchers; **33%** are using **review sites** when deciding where to go out for food and drink and **37%** of consumers are using **social media** when deciding where to eat and drink.

Web influence

Visits to bars increased by **17.9%** year-on-year to **3.3** outings per month.

Members of **Generation Y** visited bars on **1.1** more occasions than the national average.

Bars

Visits to pubs increased by **9.5%** year-on-year to **4.6** outings per month.

Generation Y visit pubs the most with an average of **3.8** outings for a drink per month, and **2.8** outings to eat in a pub.

Pubs

UK consumers go out **1.6** times per month to casual dining restaurants, an increase of **24.6% over the previous year.**

For **Generation Y** the increase is **42.8%** – that's **2.7** outings per month. This is predicted to increase by **7.5%**.

Dining

Source: Taste of the Nation, Deloitte Summer 2012
www.deloitte.com

SEE ALSO:
www.completeissues.co.uk

Fairer trade

59% of consumers feel they can make a difference through their shopping choices

What is FAIRTRADE?

The FAIRTRADE Mark is an independent consumer label which appears on UK products as a guarantee that they meet internationally agreed Fairtrade standards. It shares these standards with movements in 21 other countries.

The FAIRTRADE Foundation has licensed over 3,000 products for sale in the UK.

WORLDWIDE:

Despite worldwide financial issues, a recent global survey of 17,000 consumers shows that public support for Fairtrade continues to rise. Shoppers are increasingly expecting businesses to be more accountable and fair in dealing with producers in developing countries.

People are backing their beliefs with positive action – worldwide shoppers spent €4.36 billion (about £3.5bn) on Fairtrade products in 2010, an increase of 28%.

UK:

In the UK despite the difficult economic times half of consumers say that they regularly purchase Fairtrade products at least once a month.

% of people who have trust in Fairtrade, 2011
(all those who answered 3-4 on a trust level of 1-4 where 4= a lot of trust)

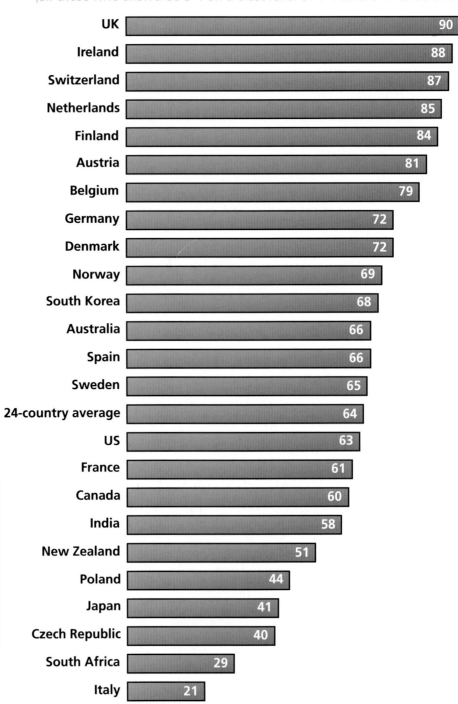

UK	90
Ireland	88
Switzerland	87
Netherlands	85
Finland	84
Austria	81
Belgium	79
Germany	72
Denmark	72
Norway	69
South Korea	68
Australia	66
Spain	66
Sweden	65
24-country average	64
US	63
France	61
Canada	60
India	58
New Zealand	51
Poland	44
Japan	41
Czech Republic	40
South Africa	29
Italy	21

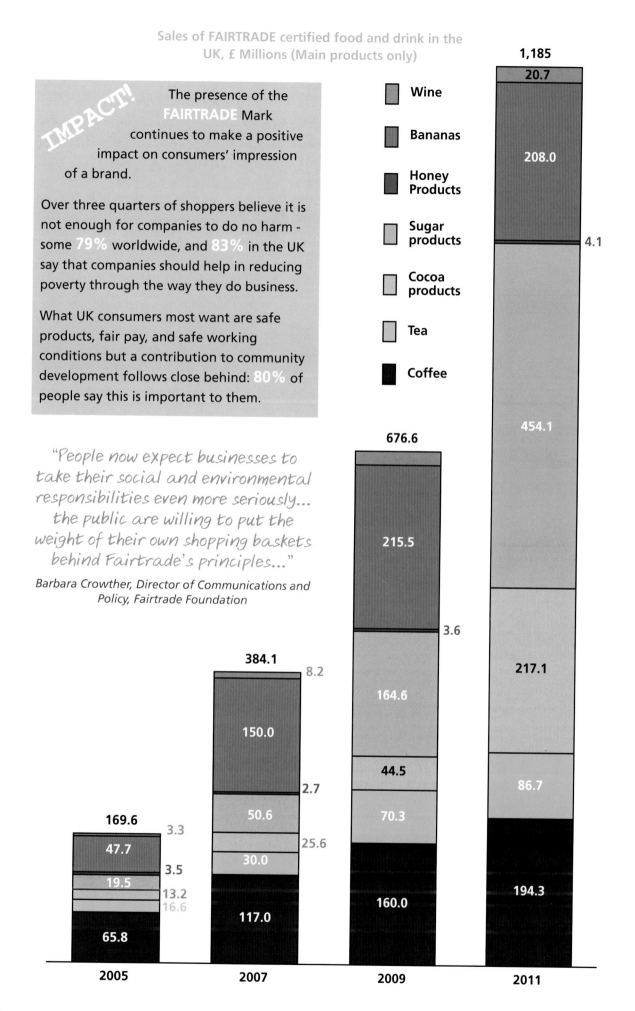

Sales of FAIRTRADE certified food and drink in the UK, £ Millions (Main products only)

IMPACT!

The presence of the **FAIRTRADE** Mark continues to make a positive impact on consumers' impression of a brand.

Over three quarters of shoppers believe it is not enough for companies to do no harm - some **79%** worldwide, and **83%** in the UK say that companies should help in reducing poverty through the way they do business.

What UK consumers most want are safe products, fair pay, and safe working conditions but a contribution to community development follows close behind: **80%** of people say this is important to them.

"People now expect businesses to take their social and environmental responsibilities even more seriously... the public are willing to put the weight of their own shopping baskets behind Fairtrade's principles..."

Barbara Crowther, Director of Communications and Policy, Fairtrade Foundation

Legend:
- Wine
- Bananas
- Honey Products
- Sugar products
- Cocoa products
- Tea
- Coffee

2005 — 169.6
- 3.3
- 47.7
- 3.5
- 19.5
- 13.2
- 16.6
- 65.8

2007 — 384.1
- 8.2
- 150.0
- 2.7
- 50.6
- 25.6
- 30.0
- 117.0

2009 — 676.6
- 215.5
- 3.6
- 164.6
- 44.5
- 70.3
- 160.0

2011 — 1,185
- 20.7
- 208.0
- 4.1
- 454.1
- 217.1
- 86.7
- 194.3

Source: Fairtrade International & GlobeScan
www.fairtrade.net

SEE ALSO:
www.completeissues.co.uk

Meat free meals

One vegetarian meal a week could help the environment

Animals kept for food produce **18%** of global greenhouse gas emissions including some of the most dangerous ones – methane and nitrous oxide.

Nearly **8%** of the water humans use goes to grow food for cattle.

A 500g packet of beef (the amount used for spaghetti bolognaise for four people) takes **6,810 litres** of water to produce.

500g of beans (the amount of beans to make bean burgers for four people) only takes **818 litres** of water.

So eating a vegetarian meal once a week could have an effect, if enough of us would do it.

Oxfam chose three developed countries and three developing countries to focus on. The countries are not 'representative' of the world, but they are illustrative.

"How comfortable would you feel about feeding your family a meat-free meal once a week?"
(Base: 4,854)

% who said they would feel [ ] **Very comfortable** [ ] **Fairly comfortable**

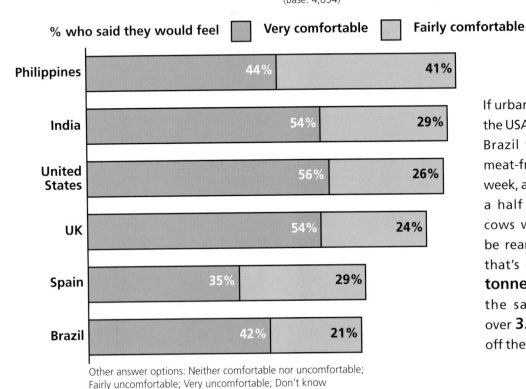

Country	Very comfortable	Fairly comfortable
Philippines	44%	41%
India	54%	29%
United States	56%	26%
UK	54%	24%
Spain	35%	29%
Brazil	42%	21%

Other answer options: Neither comfortable nor uncomfortable; Fairly uncomfortable; Very uncomfortable; Don't know

If urban households in the USA, UK, Spain and Brazil were to eat a meat-free meal once a week, around nine and a half million fewer cows would need to be reared every year: that's over **900,000 tonnes** less methane, the same as taking over **3.7 million** cars off the road for a year.

The Food Transformation, Oxfam, 2012
www.oxfam.org.uk

SEE ALSO:
www.completeissues.co.uk

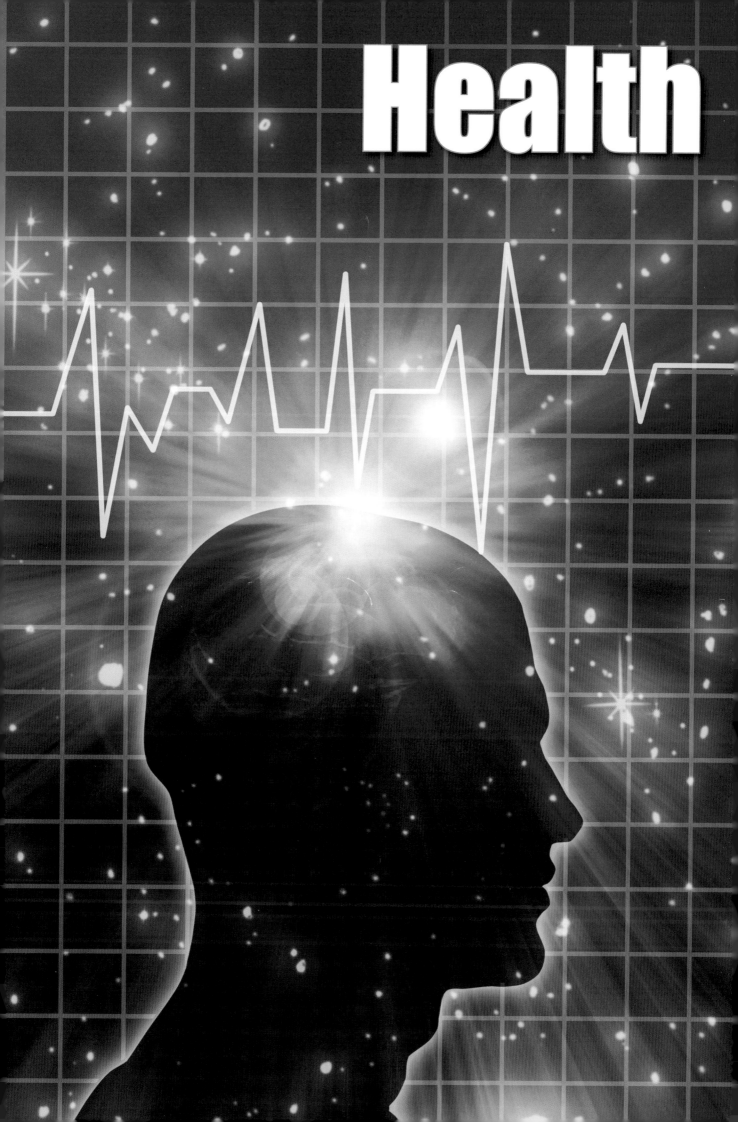

Health

How are you?

International research has revealed differences in attitudes to health

What people said about their health

(Base: Interviews with 13,373 adult members of the general public aged 18+ across 12 countries in 2011)

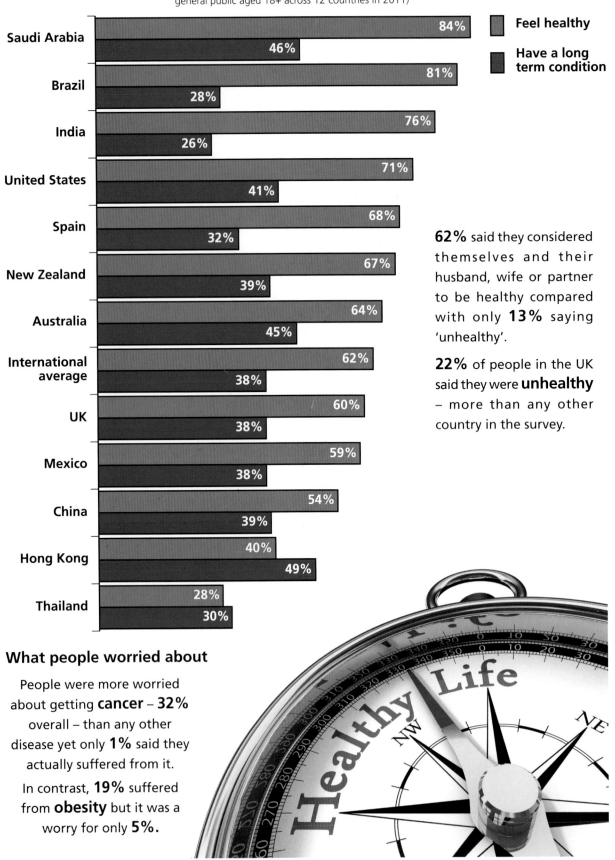

- **Feel healthy**
- **Have a long term condition**

Country	Feel healthy	Have a long term condition
Saudi Arabia	84%	46%
Brazil	81%	28%
India	76%	26%
United States	71%	41%
Spain	68%	32%
New Zealand	67%	39%
Australia	64%	45%
International average	62%	38%
UK	60%	38%
Mexico	59%	38%
China	54%	39%
Hong Kong	40%	49%
Thailand	28%	30%

62% said they considered themselves and their husband, wife or partner to be healthy compared with only **13%** saying 'unhealthy'.

22% of people in the UK said they were **unhealthy** – more than any other country in the survey.

What people worried about

People were more worried about getting **cancer** – **32%** overall – than any other disease yet only **1%** said they actually suffered from it.

In contrast, **19%** suffered from **obesity** but it was a worry for only **5%**.

Why people want to live healthily

Although internationally the main reasons for wanting to live healthily were to avoid getting ill and to feel happier, in the **US** the main reason was to **live longer**, 23%.

Overall, **73%** of respondents said health and wellbeing was their highest priority.

New Zealand, **61%** – and the UK – **62%** are at the bottom of this scale.

The countries who rated keeping their **independence** highest were **Saudi Arabia – 28%** and the **UK – 17%**

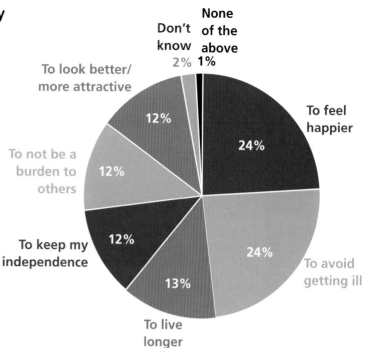

Don't know 2%

None of the above 1%

To look better/more attractive 12%

To feel happier 24%

To not be a burden to others 12%

To avoid getting ill 24%

To keep my independence 12%

To live longer 13%

Barriers to living healthier lives

62% of people said they would like to exercise more, **54%** would like a healthier diet and **52%** would like to lose weight.

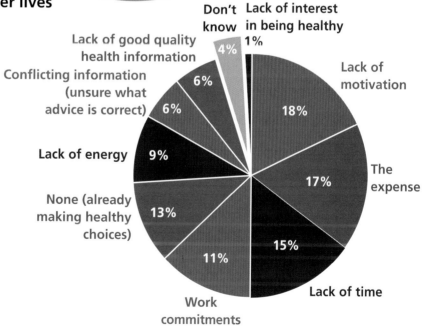

Don't know 4%

Lack of interest in being healthy 1%

Lack of good quality health information 6%

Conflicting information (unsure what advice is correct) 6%

Lack of motivation 18%

Lack of energy 9%

The expense 17%

None (already making healthy choices) 13%

Work commitments 11%

Lack of time 15%

Source: BUPA Healthpulse International Healthcare Survey 2011
www.bupa.com

SEE ALSO:
www.completeissues.co.uk

Over exposed

In Great Britain thirty years ago, skin cancer was the 17th most common cancer among people in their fifties... now it is the 5th

---

About skin cancer

There are two main types of skin cancer: **malignant melanoma** which is less common but more serious; and **non-melanoma** skin cancer, which is very common but not so serious.

For people in their fifties there were **fewer than 500 cases** each year 30 years ago, now there are **almost 2,000.**

Over this time, rates of malignant melanoma in Britain have risen faster than any of the current top ten cancers.

This sharp increase means that **more than five people a day** in this age group are now diagnosed with cancer that can prove fatal if not spotted early.

"Melanoma is a largely preventable disease; people can reduce their chance of developing skin cancer in the first place if they protect their skin from sunburn."

Sara Hiom, Director of information at Cancer Research UK

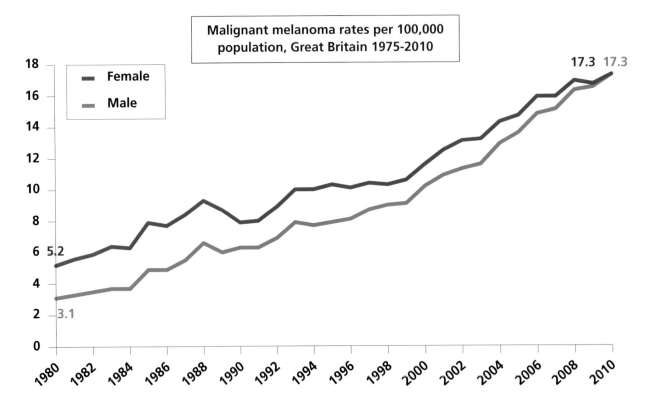

Malignant melanoma rates per 100,000 population, Great Britain 1975-2010

How common is skin cancer?

Like most cancers, skin cancer is more common among older people. But malignant melanoma is particularly high in younger people.

More than **one third** of all cases of malignant melanomas occur in people under 55.

It is almost twice as common in young women up to the age of 34 as in young men, but more men die from it.

Malignant melanoma rates per 100,000 population by age and gender, Great Britain 2008-2010

Men   Women

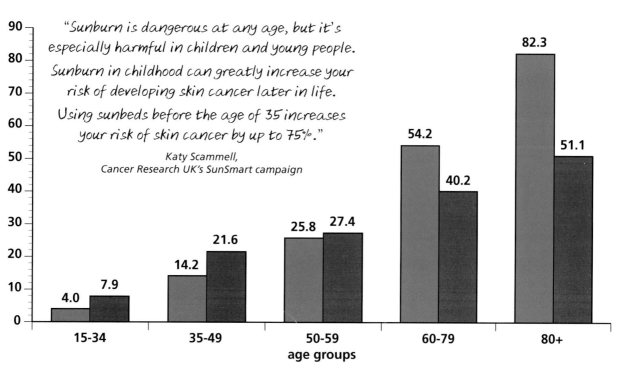

"Sunburn is dangerous at any age, but it's especially harmful in children and young people. Sunburn in childhood can greatly increase your risk of developing skin cancer later in life. Using sunbeds before the age of 35 increases your risk of skin cancer by up to 75%."

Katy Scammell,
Cancer Research UK's SunSmart campaign

age groups	Men	Women
15-34	4.0	7.9
35-49	14.2	21.6
50-59	25.8	27.4
60-79	54.2	40.2
80+	82.3	51.1

How many people survive skin cancer?

Survival rates have been improving for the last twenty-five years and are now amongst the highest for any cancer.

The latest malignant melanoma survival rates show that **84%** of men and **92%** of women survive the disease for at last five years after diagnosis.

NB 2010 figures: Because of the complex processes involved, there is usually a delay of around 18 months before cancer data is complete enough to be published

Source: Cancer Research UK
www.cancerresearchuk.org
www.sunsmart.org.uk

The most common area for men to develop malignant melanoma is on the chest or back.

For women it is on the legs.

SEE ALSO:
www.completeissues.co.uk

Desperate thoughts

If we set aside the myths about suicide, we may have a better understanding of it

MYTH: YOU HAVE TO BE MENTALLY ILL TO EVEN THINK ABOUT SUICIDE

FACT: Most people have thought of suicide from time to time. However, many people who kill themselves do have mental health problems. Sometimes this is recognised before the person's death.

MYTH: PEOPLE WHO TALK ABOUT SUICIDE AREN'T REALLY SERIOUS AND NOT LIKELY TO ACTUALLY KILL THEMSELVES

FACT: People who kill themselves have often told someone that they do not feel life is worth living or that they have no future. Some may have actually said they want to die – it is very important that everyone who says they feel suicidal be treated seriously.

In **20.3%** of all written or spoken contact to Samaritans the caller expressed suicidal feelings at the time of the call

Samaritans: 08457 909090

MYTH: ONCE A PERSON HAS MADE A SERIOUS SUICIDE ATTEMPT, THAT PERSON IS UNLIKELY TO MAKE ANOTHER

FACT: People who have attempted to kill themselves are significantly more likely to eventually die by suicide than the rest of the population.

MYTH: IF A PERSON IS SERIOUS ABOUT KILLING THEMSELVES THEN THERE IS NOTHING YOU CAN DO

FACT: Feeling suicidal is often a temporary state of mind. Whilst someone may feel low or distressed for a sustained period the actual suicidal crisis can be relatively short term.

MYTH: TALKING ABOUT SUICIDE IS A BAD IDEA AS IT MAY GIVE SOMEONE THE IDEA TO TRY IT

FACT: By asking directly about suicide you give that person permission to tell you how they feel – people often say that it was a huge relief to be able to talk about their suicidal thoughts. Once someone starts talking they have a greater chance of discovering other options to suicide.

MYTH: MOST SUICIDES HAPPEN IN THE WINTER MONTHS

FACT: Suicide is more common in the spring and summer months.

MYTH: PEOPLE WHO THREATEN SUICIDE ARE JUST ATTENTION SEEKING AND SHOULDN'T BE TAKEN SERIOUSLY

FACT: People may well talk about their feelings because they want support in dealing with them. In this sense it may be that they do indeed want attention in which case giving that attention may save their life.

MYTH: PEOPLE WHO ARE SUICIDAL WANT TO DIE

FACT: The majority do not actually want to die; they just do not want to live the life they have. This important fact means it is vital to talk through other options at the right time.

In **42.9%** of email contacts and **52.2%** of text contacts to Samaritans the caller expressed suicidal feelings at that time

Suicidal thoughts

CALM – The Campaign Against Living Miserably surveyed nearly 1,000 adults in England and Wales.

25% of adults have considered suicide

30% of 25-34 year olds have thought about ending their life

53% of those who considered suicide did so fairly or very seriously

28% of women have had suicidal thoughts compared to **22%** of men

However statistics show that **three times** as many men as women take their own lives each year

The survey revealed that a key factor likely to increase suicidal thoughts was **relationship status:**

36% of respondents who had been separated or divorced had considered suicide

compared with lower rates for those:

living as married **27%**, married or in a civil partnership **22%**, never married **26%** and widowed **23%**

The number of children in the household

also appears to have an impact:

33% of those in a household with three or more children had experienced suicidal thoughts

compared to:

25% in two children households and **23%** in homes with just one child

Source: Samaritans; CALM – The Campaign Against Living Miserably
www.samaritans.org
www.thecalmzone.net

SEE ALSO:
Suicide, p114-115
www.completeissues.co.uk

Suicide

There are approximately three times more male than female suicides in the UK

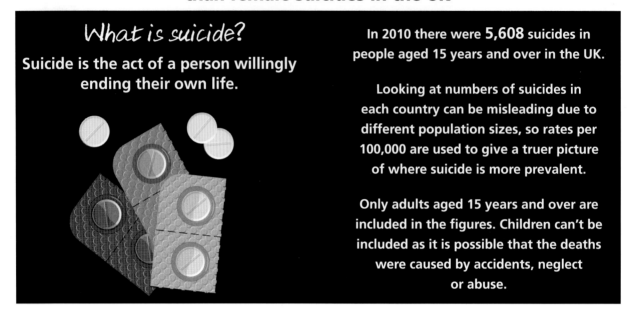

What is suicide?

Suicide is the act of a person willingly ending their own life.

In 2010 there were **5,608** suicides in people aged 15 years and over in the UK.

Looking at numbers of suicides in each country can be misleading due to different population sizes, so rates per 100,000 are used to give a truer picture of where suicide is more prevalent.

Only adults aged 15 years and over are included in the figures. Children can't be included as it is possible that the deaths were caused by accidents, neglect or abuse.

In 2010, the highest suicide rate per 100,000 for **males** was in Northern Ireland, the lowest was in England.

The highest rate per 100,000 for females was also in Northern Ireland, the lowest was in Wales.

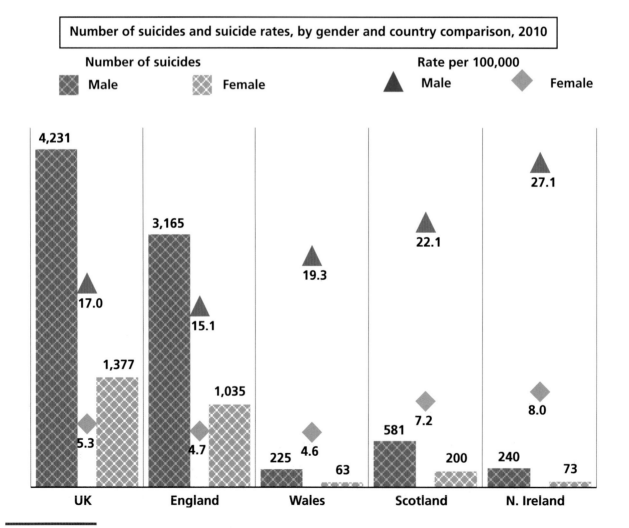

Number of suicides and suicide rates, by gender and country comparison, 2010

Number of suicides
- Male
- Female

Rate per 100,000
- ▲ Male
- ◆ Female

	UK	England	Wales	Scotland	N. Ireland
Male number	4,231	3,165	225	581	240
Female number	1,377	1,035	63	200	73
Male rate	17.0	15.1	19.3	22.1	27.1
Female rate	5.3	4.7	4.6	7.2	8.0

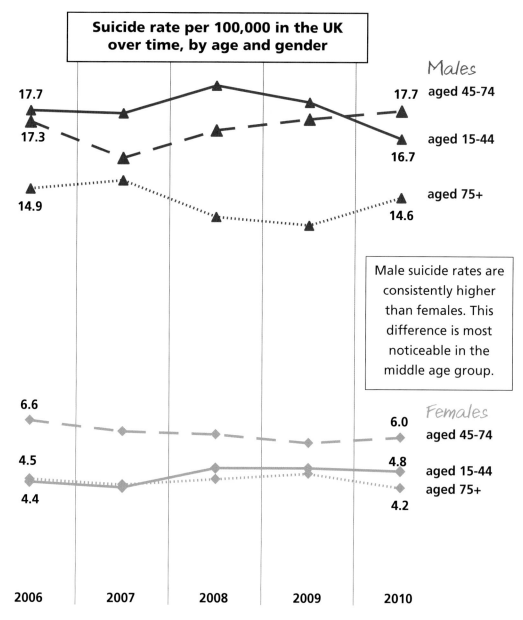

Suicide rate per 100,000 in the UK over time, by age and gender

Males

17.7 — aged 45-74 — 17.7

17.3 — aged 15-44 — 16.7

14.9 — aged 75+ — 14.6

Male suicide rates are consistently higher than females. This difference is most noticeable in the middle age group.

Females

6.6 — aged 45-74 — 6.0

4.5 — aged 15-44 — 4.8

4.4 — aged 75+ — 4.2

2006   2007   2008   2009   2010

Why do people take their own lives?

You can feel suicidal for all sorts of reasons, eg:

- Something might have happened to you that has upset you a great deal.

- When someone close to you has attempted or actually committed suicide.

- You have been using drugs or drinking heavily.

- You may be upset and angry for no reason at all.

- A combination of any of these things.

Samaritans: 08457 909090

Source: Samaritans; Office for National Statistics © Crown copyright 2012; CALM – The Campaign Against Living Miserably
www.samaritans.org
www.ons.gov.uk
www.thecalmzone.net

SEE ALSO:
Desperate thoughts, p112-113

www.completeissues.co.uk

Blood bank

1.6 million people donated blood in the last year

Although that sounds a lot, that's only 4% of the population, giving two or three times a year.

This amounts to 2.1 million donations. Anyone who is generally in good health, aged 17 to 65 can donate.

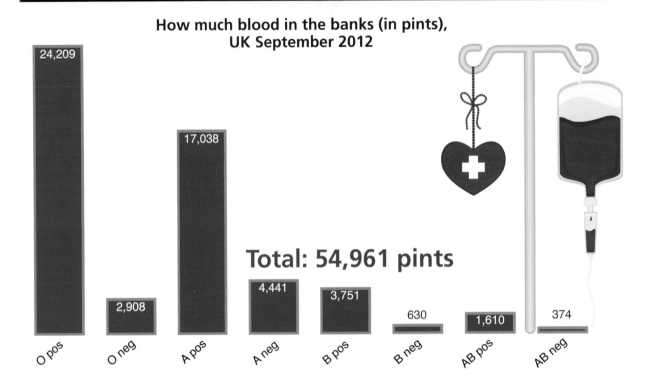

How much blood in the banks (in pints), UK September 2012

Total: 54,961 pints

O pos	O neg	A pos	A neg	B pos	B neg	AB pos	AB neg
24,209	2,908	17,038	4,441	3,751	630	1,610	374

A regular supply of blood is vital. Red cells which carry blood around the body last only 35 days. Platelets, the tiny cells that help your blood to clot only survive for 5 days.

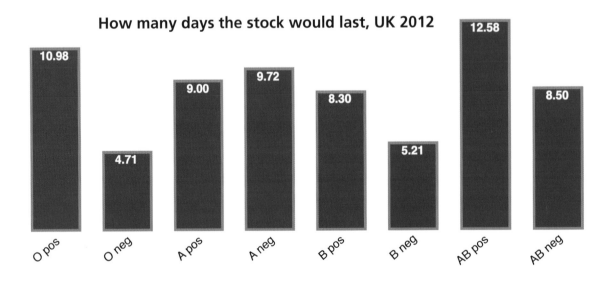

How many days the stock would last, UK 2012

O pos	O neg	A pos	A neg	B pos	B neg	AB pos	AB neg
10.98	4.71	9.00	9.72	8.30	5.21	12.58	8.50

Source: The National Blood Service 2012
www.blood.co.uk

SEE ALSO:
www.completeissues.co.uk

http://www

Internet
& media

Media trust

Despite media scandals, trust has actually increased

The Edelman Trust survey, is an annual exercise which surveys 25,000 people in 25 countries. Their survey focuses on the 'informed public' (college-educated; household income in the top quartile for their age in their country; read or watch business/news media at least several times a week).

They were asked about their trust in the media, government and business. The results show that while people in the UK are increasingly sceptical about politicians and business leaders, trust in the media has increased

Percentage of people WORLDWIDE who have trust in the different types of organisations

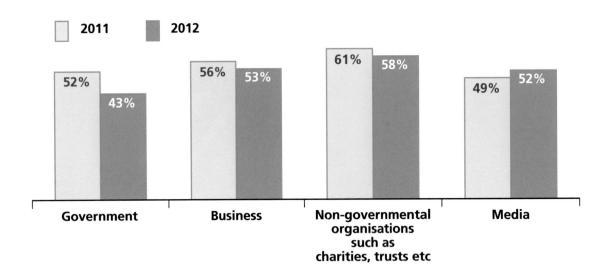

☐ 2011 ■ 2012

Government	Business	Non-governmental organisations such as charities, trusts etc	Media
52% / 43%	56% / 53%	61% / 58%	49% / 52%

Percentage of people WORLDWIDE who have trust in the different types of media

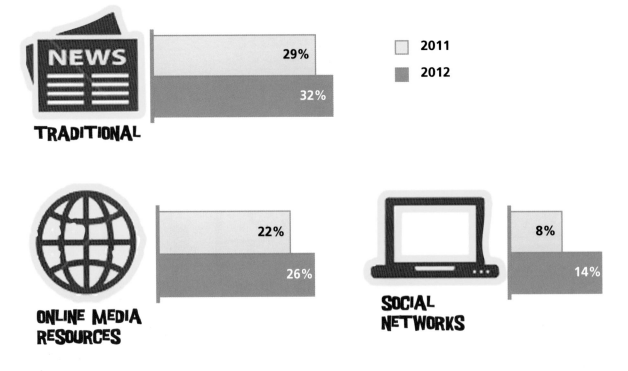

TRADITIONAL — 29% (2011), 32% (2012)

☐ 2011
■ 2012

ONLINE MEDIA RESOURCES — 22% (2011), 26% (2012)

SOCIAL NETWORKS — 8% (2011), 14% (2012)

Percentage of people WORLDWIDE who have trust in the media

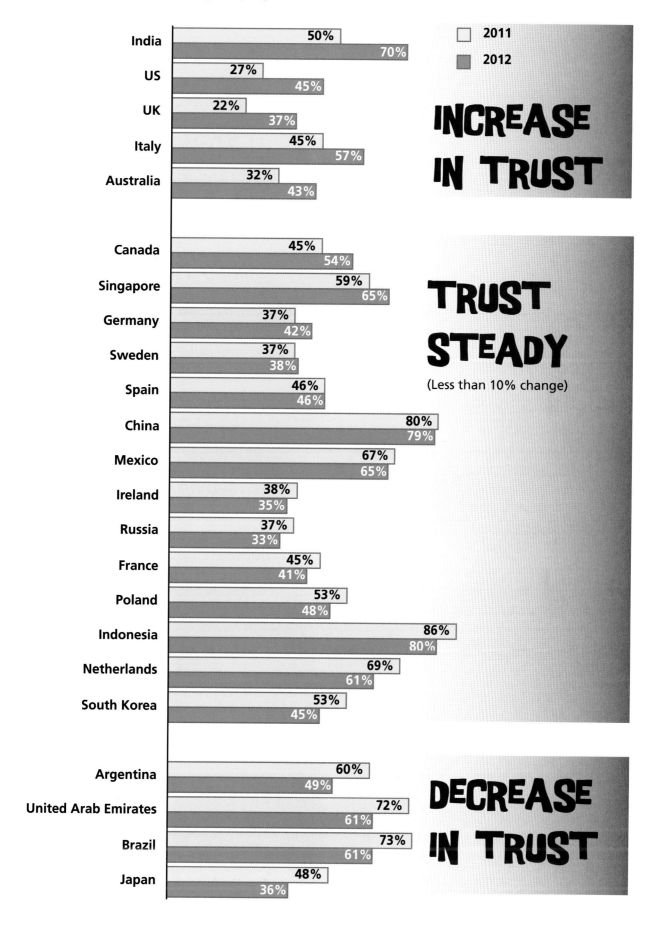

Legend:
- ☐ 2011
- ▨ 2012

INCREASE IN TRUST

Country	2011	2012
India	50%	70%
US	27%	45%
UK	22%	37%
Italy	45%	57%
Australia	32%	43%

TRUST STEADY (Less than 10% change)

Country	2011	2012
Canada	45%	54%
Singapore	59%	65%
Germany	37%	42%
Sweden	37%	38%
Spain	46%	46%
China	80%	79%
Mexico	67%	65%
Ireland	38%	35%
Russia	37%	33%
France	45%	41%
Poland	53%	48%
Indonesia	86%	80%
Netherlands	69%	61%
South Korea	53%	45%

DECREASE IN TRUST

Country	2011	2012
Argentina	60%	49%
United Arab Emirates	72%	61%
Brazil	73%	61%
Japan	48%	36%

Source: Edelman Trust Barometer
trust.edelman.com

SEE ALSO:
www.completeissues.co.uk

Friend... or stranger?

As children's use of the internet increases – so too does risk

A study of **25,142** children aged 9-16, who use the internet, along with one of their parents, in 25 European countries found that:

60%
go online **every day** or **almost every day**

30%
of the children studied had **communicated** online with someone they have not met face to face.

93%
go online **at least weekly**

Only **9%**
had met online contacts. **Half** had met **one or two** people in the past year, **half** had met **more**.

Online activity can benefit, but it can be harmful too. Children can experiment online with relationships, intimacy and identity but these opportunities can also be risks

40%
had looked for new friends on the internet

16%
had pretended to be a different kind of person on the internet from what they really are

34%
have added people to their friends list or address book that they had never met face to face

15%
had sent personal information to someone that they had never met face to face

14%
had sent a photo or video of themselves to someone that they had never met face to face

There is general public anxiety over meeting strangers (as adults see it) and making new friends (as children see it)

The children studied were asked had they...

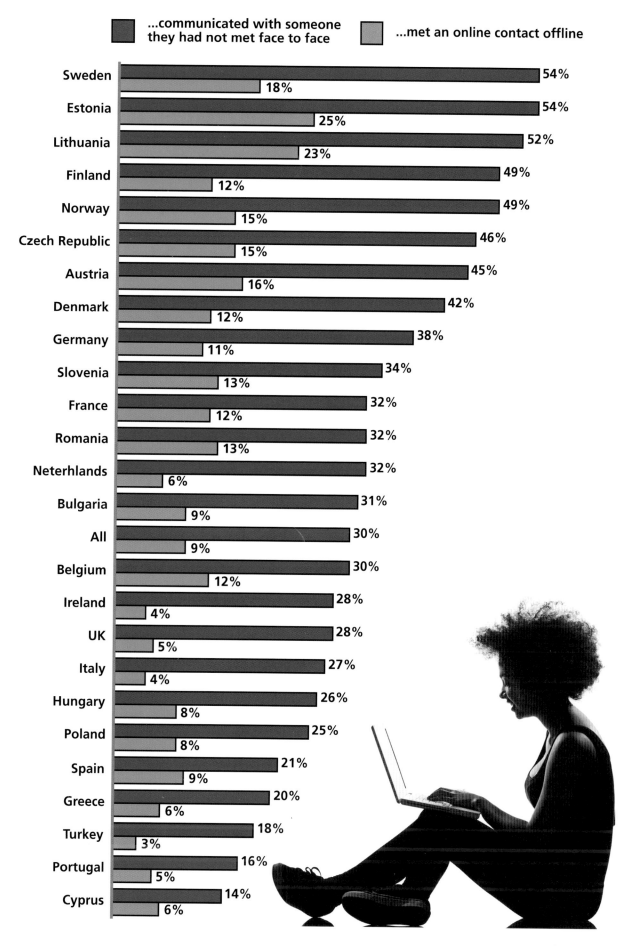

■ ...communicated with someone they had not met face to face
■ ...met an online contact offline

Country	Communicated	Met offline
Sweden	54%	18%
Estonia	54%	25%
Lithuania	52%	23%
Finland	49%	12%
Norway	49%	15%
Czech Republic	46%	15%
Austria	45%	16%
Denmark	42%	12%
Germany	38%	11%
Slovenia	34%	13%
France	32%	12%
Romania	32%	13%
Neterhlands	32%	6%
Bulgaria	31%	9%
All	30%	9%
Belgium	30%	12%
Ireland	28%	4%
UK	28%	5%
Italy	27%	4%
Hungary	26%	8%
Poland	25%	8%
Spain	21%	9%
Greece	20%	6%
Turkey	18%	3%
Portugal	16%	5%
Cyprus	14%	6%

Source: EU Kids Online Survey
www.eukidsonline.net
www2.lse.ac.uk

SEE ALSO:
At risk?, p122-123
www.completeissues.co.uk

At risk?

Myths about internet use and safety over-simplify what is actually happening

A study in 25 European countries of **25,142** children aged 9-16, who use the internet, along with one of their parents, showed the reality.

The top 10 myths about children's online risks

Myth: Digital natives* know it all

Only **36%** of 9-16 year-olds say it is very true that they know more about the internet than their parents.

Myth: Everyone is creating their own content

The study showed that only **one in five** children had recently used a file-sharing site or created a pet or an avatar, **half that number** wrote a blog. Most children use the internet for ready-made content.

Myth: Under 13s can't use social networking sites

Although many sites eg Facebook, say that users must be aged at least 13, the survey shows that age limits don't work – **38%** of 9-12 year-olds have a social networking profile.

Myth: Everyone watches porn online

One in seven children saw sexual images online in the past year. Even allowing for under-reporting, this myth has been partly created by media hype.

Myth: Bullies are baddies

The study shows that **60%** who bully (online or offline) have themselves been bullied. Bullies and victims are often the same people.

Myth: People you meet on the internet are strangers

87% of online contacts are people children know face-to-face. **9%** met offline people they'd first contacted online – most didn't go alone and only **1%** had a bad experience.

Myth: Offline risks migrate online

Children who report more risk offline are more likely to report risks online. It cannot be assumed that those who are low-risk offline are not exposed while online.

Myth: Putting the PC in the living room will help

Children find it so easy to go online at a friend's house or on a smartphone that this advice is out of date. Parents should talk to their children about their internet habits or join them in some online activity.

Myth: Teaching digital skills reduces online risk

The more digital skills a child has, the more risks they are likely to encounter as they broaden their online experience. Some skills could reduce the harm that children are exposed to.

Myth: Children can get around safety software

Fewer than **one in three** 11-16 year-olds say they can change filter preferences. And most say their parents' action to limit their internet use is helpful.

*a person who was born during or after the general introduction of digital technology, and has used it from an early age

What risks?

40% of the children surveyed encountered one or more forms of online risk in the past year.

14% had seen sexual images; **30%** had contact online with someone they had not met face-to-face; **6%** had been sent a nasty or hurtful message/been bullied online.

15% have seen or received sexual messages online.

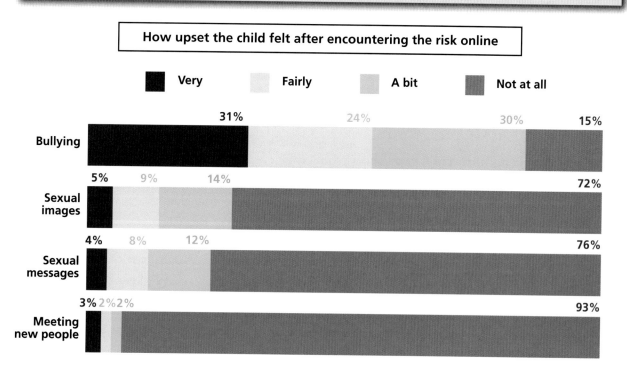

How upset the child felt after encountering the risk online

■ Very ▢ Fairly ▢ A bit ▢ Not at all

Bullying
31% | 24% | 30% | 15%

Sexual images
5% | 9% | 14% | 72%

Sexual messages
4% | 8% | 12% | 76%

Meeting new people
3% 2% 2% | 93%

How did they cope with bullying?

Being bullied online was the risk that upset children the most, even though it was among the least common.

Some children tried to fix the problem, most told someone, usually a friend but often a parent, and other children blocked the person sending the hurtful messages.

" ...the digital world brings both risks and opportunities for young people... risk isn't automatically a bad thing as it may give children a chance to learn how to cope **"**

Professor Sonia Livingstone

Source: EU Kids Online Survey
www.eukidsonline.net
www2.lse.ac.uk

SEE ALSO:
Friend... or stranger?, p120-121
www.completeissues.co.uk

Cyber safe

"Cybercriminals must not be allowed to disrupt our use of the internet..."

Concerns

What concerns do you have, if any, about using the internet for things like online banking or buying things online?
(Base: 18,881 Internet users in the EU27)

Someone taking/misusing your personal data — **40%**

Security of online payments — **38%**

Prefer conducting transaction in person eg so you can inspect the product yourself or ask a real person about them — **24%**

Not receiving the goods or services that you buy online — **19%**

Other — **4%**

None — **21%**

Don't know — **2%**

This was the biggest concern in **Germany 59%** and **Luxembourg 54%**

The respondents most concerned about this were in the **UK 56%** and **France 50%**

40% of internet users in **Denmark, 36%** in both **Sweden** and **Poland, 35%** in **Estonia**, and **33%** in both **Austria** and **Latvia**, have **no concerns** over online banking or buying things online

Behaviour

Internet users in the EU have changed their behaviour in a number of ways because of security concerns:

51% have installed anti-virus software

43% don't open emails from people they don't know

37% are less likely to give personal information on websites

34% only visit websites they know and trust

29% only use their own computer

25% use different passwords for different sites

18% were less likely to buy goods online

16% have changed their security settings

15% are less likely to bank online

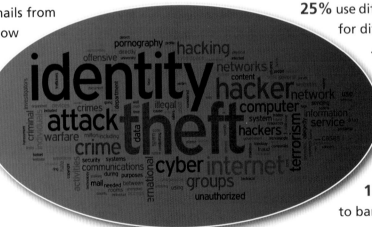

"...The more we know about the risks and how to protect ourselves, the more we can truly maximise our digital lives"
Cecilia Malmström, EU Commissioner for Home Affairs

Experiences

How often have you experienced or been a victim of the following situations?
(Base: 18,881 Internet users in the EU27)

■ **Often**   ■ **Occasionally**   ■ **Never**   ■ **Don't know**

Received emails fraudulently asking for money or personal details (inc banking or payment information)
10% | 28% | 61% | 1%

Accidentally encountering material which promotes racial hatred or religious extremism
2% | 13% | 83% | 2%

Not being able to access online services (eg banking services) because of cyber attacks
1% | 12% | 85% | 2%

Online fraud where goods purchased were not delivered, counterfeit or not as advertised
1% | 11% | 86% | 2%

Identity theft (someone stealing your personal data and impersonating you (eg shopping under your name)
1% | 7% | 90% | 2%

54% of respondents in both **Denmark** and **the Netherlands** and **52%** in the **UK** say that they have **received emails fraudulently asking for money and personal details.**

The **least likely to receive scam emails** were in **Bulgaria** and **Greece**, both **18%.**

16% of internet users in **Romania** and **12%** in both **Hungary** and the **UK**, say they have experienced **identity theft**, all higher than the EU average of **8%.**

The **lowest levels** are in **Slovenia** and **Lithuania**, both **2%.**

The **highest experience of online fraud** was in **Poland, 18%, Hungary, 17% Malta** and the **UK**, both **16%.**

The **least likely** are **Greece, 3%, Slovenia, 6%** and **Spain, 7%.**

CYBER CRIME

Source: © European Commission – Special Eurobarometer 390 – Cyber Security Report 2012
ec.europa.eu/public_opinion/index_en.htm

SEE ALSO:
EU online, p126-127
www.completeissues.co.uk

EU online

Internet activity varies considerably by country

How often do you access the internet?
(eg for sending emails, reading online news, chatting with friends or buying products online)
(Base: 26,593 respondents in EU27)

Several times a day	39%
Once a day	14%
Several times a week	10%
Once a week	3%
Several times a month	2%
Once a month	1%
Less often	2%
Never	29%

The Netherlands, Denmark and Sweden have the highest level of internet use – 83% in each country accessing the internet **at least once a day**.

63% of people in the UK access the internet **at least once a day**.

Portugal had the highest proportion **never** using the internet– 58%.

Where do you access the internet?
(Base: 18,881 respondents who ever use the internet)

Access

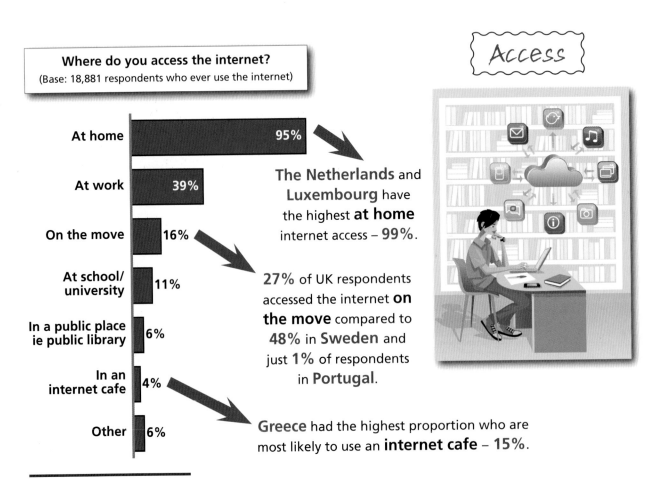

At home	95%
At work	39%
On the move	16%
At school/ university	11%
In a public place ie public library	6%
In an internet cafe	4%
Other	6%

The Netherlands and Luxembourg have the highest **at home** internet access – 99%.

27% of UK respondents accessed the internet **on the move** compared to 48% in Sweden and just 1% of respondents in Portugal.

Greece had the highest proportion who are most likely to use an **internet cafe** – 15%.

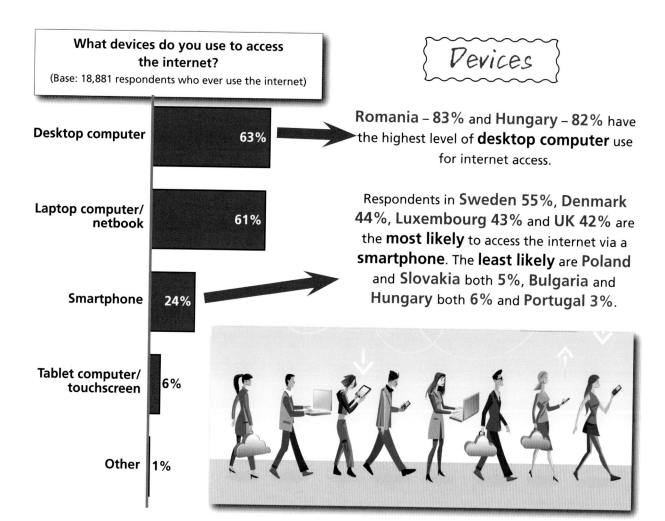

What devices do you use to access the internet?
(Base: 18,881 respondents who ever use the internet)

- Desktop computer — **63%**
- Laptop computer/netbook — **61%**
- Smartphone — **24%**
- Tablet computer/touchscreen — **6%**
- Other — **1%**

Romania – 83% and **Hungary – 82%** have the highest level of **desktop computer** use for internet access.

Respondents in **Sweden 55%**, **Denmark 44%**, **Luxembourg 43%** and **UK 42%** are the **most likely** to access the internet via a **smartphone**. The **least likely** are **Poland** and **Slovakia** both **5%**, **Bulgaria** and **Hungary** both **6%** and **Portugal 3%**.

Activities

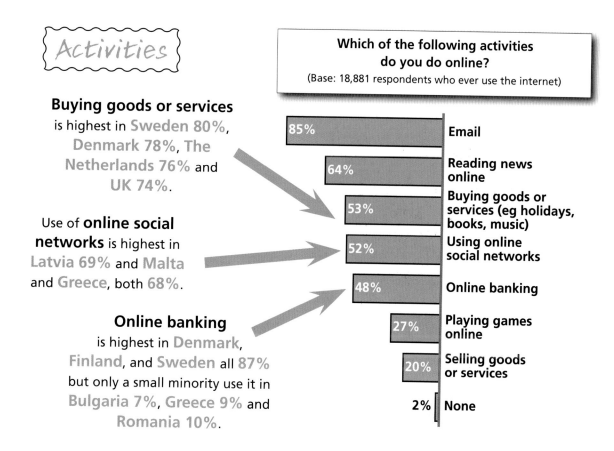

Which of the following activities do you do online?
(Base: 18,881 respondents who ever use the internet)

Buying goods or services is highest in Sweden 80%, Denmark 78%, The Netherlands 76% and UK 74%.

Use of **online social networks** is highest in Latvia 69% and Malta and Greece, both 68%.

Online banking is highest in Denmark, Finland, and Sweden all 87% but only a small minority use it in Bulgaria 7%, Greece 9% and Romania 10%.

- 85% — Email
- 64% — Reading news online
- 53% — Buying goods or services (eg holidays, books, music)
- 52% — Using online social networks
- 48% — Online banking
- 27% — Playing games online
- 20% — Selling goods or services
- 2% — None

Source: © European Commission – Special Eurobarometer 390 – Cyber Security Report 2012
ec.europa.eu/public_opinion/index_en.htm

SEE ALSO:
Cyber safe, p124-125
www.completeissues.co.uk

Your call

"Smartphones are now being used like a digital 'Swiss Army Knife', replacing possessions like watches, cameras, books and even laptops"

David Johnson, General Manager Devices for O2 in the UK

An O2 survey of 2,000 smartphone owning UK adults revealed that they spend over 2 hours a day using their phones – however, making calls comes fifth in the ranking of things they are used for:

How long we spend using our smartphones (by activity) each day	
Activity	**Mins/ day**
Browsing the internet	24.81
Checking social networks	17.49
Playing games	14.44
Listening to music	15.64
Making calls	12.13
Checking/writing emails	11.1
Text messaging	10.2
Watching TV/films	9.39
Reading books	9.3
Taking photographs	3.42
Total	**128**

% of people who use their phone for the following functions	
Function	
Taking photographs	74%
Making phone calls	71%
Text messaging	69%
Surfing the internet	69%
Alarm clock	64%
Email	52%
As a watch	50%
Using it as an address book	50%
Using social networks	49%
Use it as a diary	39%
Music	39%
Playing games	38%
Watching TV/films	22%
Reading books	13%

The phone has also started to replace a range of other possessions:

54% say they use their phones in place of an alarm clock

46% use a phone instead of a watch

39% have switched to use their phone instead of a separate camera

28% use their phone instead of a laptop

11% have replaced a games console in favour of their handset

6% use their phone in place of TV; and

6% use it instead of reading physical books

Source: Opinium Research for O2
www.o2.co.uk
www.opinium.co.uk

SEE ALSO:
www.completeissues.co.uk

Law & order

Behind the riots

Was deprivation a key factor in the riots?

The worst public disturbances since the 1980s were seen in August 2011 when there was five days of rioting in cities and towns across England.

It started with a police shooting and a peaceful protest in North London and ended up involving around 14,000 rioters.

5 deaths

90% of rioters were male

25% of rioters were students

74% rioters under age 24

People arrested known to police
9 OUT OF **10**

Youngest arrested age
10

£300m estimated damage to property

£43.5m cost of clean up

£80m lost in sales

£520m estimated cut in tourism spend

From the rioters' perspective

 Jobs aren't available or very badly paid, but the pressure to have the latest designer items is immense

They were all insured, so it didn't matter

I needed to provide for my family but a "need to" turned to greed and so I looted

It was a moment of madness – I regret it every day

It wasn't political – it was shopping

Most people got caught up watching the riots. They saw the police doing nothing and just thought they could get away with it too

All news channels were playing end-to-end coverage of the London riots. It was like an open invitation to go out and riot

There was a 50:50 chance of getting caught and the prize made it a good enough gamble

Official figures suggested that **26%** of the disturbances involved those aged 10-17 and **48%** between 18 and 24.

The Children's Society surveyed **1,077** 13 to 17 year olds and **1,004** adults in the UK about their views of the riots.

Q: **What do you think were the reasons why some young people became involved in the riots?**

(Answers were chosen from a list and more than one answer could be chosen)

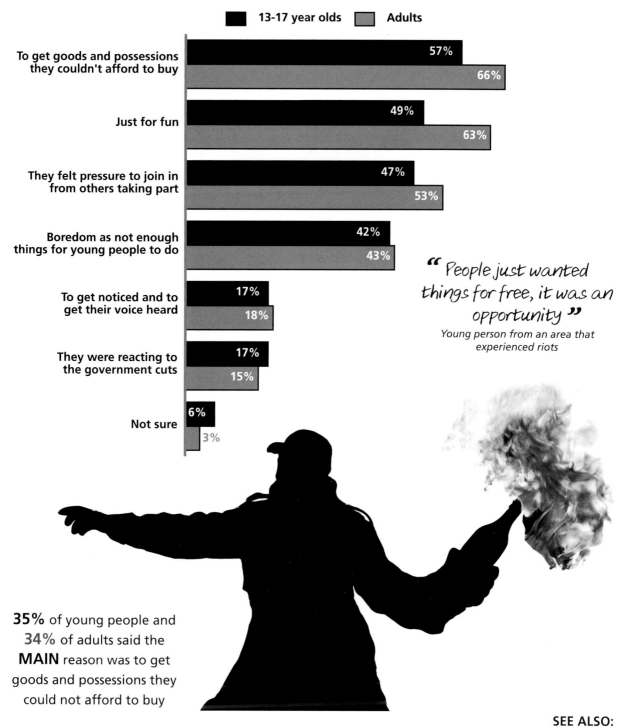

■ **13-17 year olds**   ■ **Adults**

To get goods and possessions they couldn't afford to buy
- 57%
- 66%

Just for fun
- 49%
- 63%

They felt pressure to join in from others taking part
- 47%
- 53%

Boredom as not enough things for young people to do
- 42%
- 43%

To get noticed and to get their voice heard
- 17%
- 18%

They were reacting to the government cuts
- 17%
- 15%

Not sure
- 6%
- 3%

" People just wanted things for free, it was an opportunity "
Young person from an area that experienced riots

35% of young people and **34%** of adults said the **MAIN** reason was to get goods and possessions they could not afford to buy

SEE ALSO:

I predict a riot, Fact File 2012, p120-121

Riots in England: Political protest or lawless trolley-dash, Essential Articles 15, p140

Rioters need a good therapeutic talking to, Essential Articles 15, p144

www.completeissues.co.uk

Source: *Behind the riots © The Children's Society; 5 Days in August - Riots Communities and Victims Panel*
www.childrenssociety.org.uk

Violent playgrounds

Young people suffered 586,000 incidents of violence in 2010/11

Young people's experience of crime is different from adults' in terms of *when* it takes place, *who* commits it and *where* it happens.

Where violence to children happens

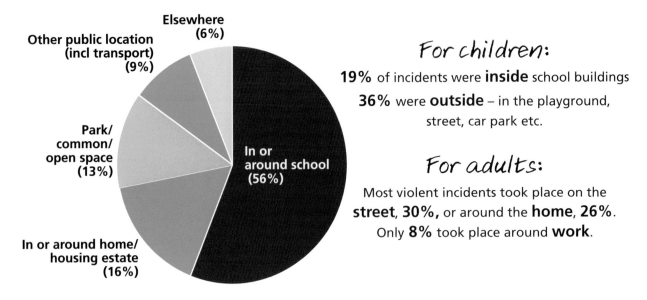

Elsewhere (6%)

Other public location (incl transport) (9%)

Park/ common/ open space (13%)

In or around home/ housing estate (16%)

In or around school (56%)

For children:

19% of incidents were **inside** school buildings

36% were **outside** – in the playground, street, car park etc.

For adults:

Most violent incidents took place on the **street, 30%,** or around the **home, 26%.** Only **8%** took place around **work.**

Who violence is committed by

Usually someone in the child's age group. **68%** of the offences were committed by someone at the same school.

■ Children aged 10 to 15   ■ Adults aged 16 or over

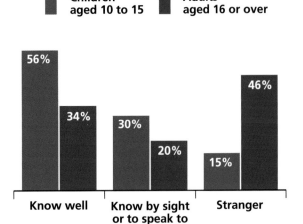

- 56% / 34% — Know well
- 30% / 20% — Know by sight or to speak to
- 15% / 46% — Stranger

When it happens

■ Children aged 10 to 15   ■ Adults aged 16 or over

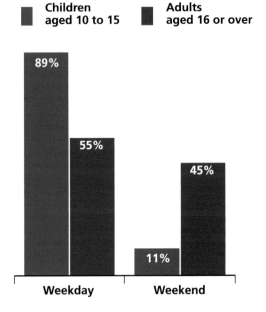

- 89% / 55% — Weekday
- 11% / 45% — Weekend

Figures may not add up due to rounding

*Violence includes wounding, robbery, assault with minor injury and assault with injury

Base: 3,859 10-15 year olds randomly selected from households taking part in the British Crime Survey.
The data is based on incidents rather than victims as some victims had been subject to more than one incident.

Who are the victims?

Among children aged 10 to 15

9.5% of boys and **4.1% of girls** had experienced violence

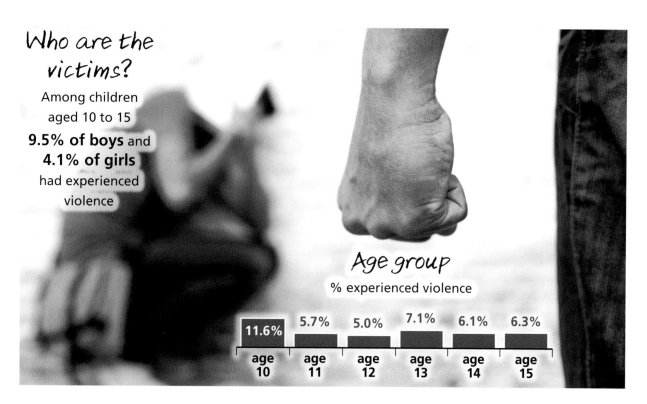

Age group
% experienced violence

age 10	age 11	age 12	age 13	age 14	age 15
11.6%	5.7%	5.0%	7.1%	6.1%	6.3%

Vulnerable children

those with a disability or who had already been bullied were more likely to be victims

% experienced violence

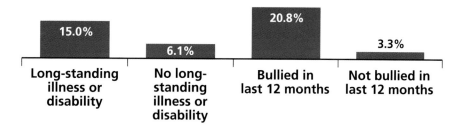

Long-standing illness or disability	No long-standing illness or disability	Bullied in last 12 months	Not bullied in last 12 months
15.0%	6.1%	20.8%	3.3%

Although **41%** of violent incidents involving **adults** are reported to the police, only **14%** of those involving these **young people** are reported.

85% of incidents that occurred around school were reported to a teacher.

Another reason is that children do not see this violence as a crime:

How children perceived the incidents

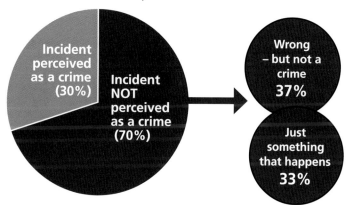

Incident perceived as a crime (30%)

Incident NOT perceived as a crime (70%)

Wrong – but not a crime **37%**

Just something that happens **33%**

Source: Hate crime, cyber security and the experience of crime among children: Findings from the 2010/11 British Crime Survey, March 2012 © Crown copyright www.homeoffice.gov.uk

SEE ALSO:
www.completeissues.co.uk

Full to bursting

59% of prisons in England and Wales are overcrowded

According to the Ministry of Justice figures (July 2012) there are 7,294 more people in the prison system than it is designed and built to hold.

The 10 most overcrowded prisons in England and Wales
(percentage overcrowded)

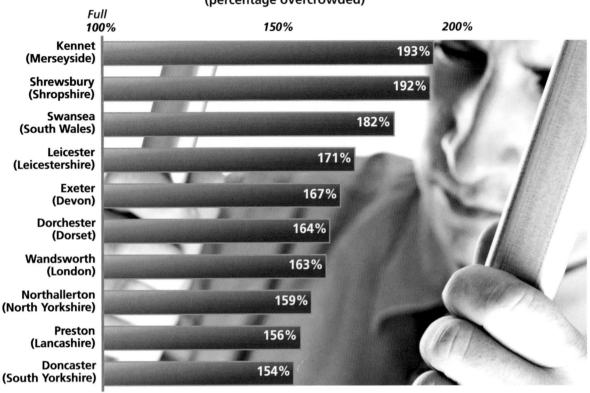

	Full 100%	150%	200%
Kennet (Merseyside)			193%
Shrewsbury (Shropshire)			192%
Swansea (South Wales)		182%	
Leicester (Leicestershire)		171%	
Exeter (Devon)		167%	
Dorchester (Dorset)		164%	
Wandsworth (London)		163%	
Northallerton (North Yorkshire)		159%	
Preston (Lancashire)		156%	
Doncaster (South Yorkshire)		154%	

The prison population is likely to increase
Projected Prison Population based on sentencing trends

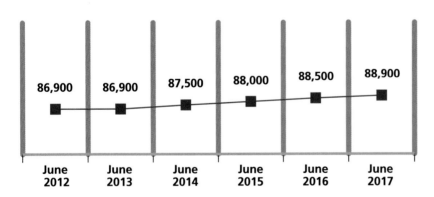

June 2012	June 2013	June 2014	June 2015	June 2016	June 2017
86,900	86,900	87,500	88,000	88,500	88,900

The average yearly cost of keeping someone in prison in 2010/11 was **£26,978.**

When overheads such as property maintenance, prisoner transportation and custody were included this rose to **£37,163**

According to the Prison Reform Trust, overcrowding makes it much harder for staff to help prisoners to reform and makes it more likely that prisoners will re-offend ● ● ●

Source: Ministry of Justice; © Crown copyright 2012;
Prison Reform Trust
www.justice.gov.uk
www.prisonreformtrust.org.uk

SEE ALSO:
www.completeissues.co.uk

No stopping them

A large number of offenders continue to commit crimes

 To help work out the best way to stop people from continuing to commit crimes, the Ministry of Justice tracked **480,000** people, who had committed an offence in the year 2000, for a period of nine years.

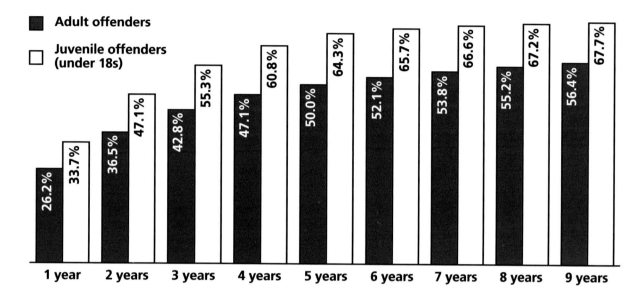

Percentage who had re-offended by end of each year of tracking period (cumulative)

Adult offenders

Juvenile offenders (under 18s)

	1 year	2 years	3 years	4 years	5 years	6 years	7 years	8 years	9 years
Adult	26.2%	36.5%	42.8%	47.1%	50.0%	52.1%	53.8%	55.2%	56.4%
Juvenile	33.7%	47.1%	55.3%	60.8%	64.3%	65.7%	66.6%	67.2%	67.7%

Of the **480,000 offenders**, **54,108** had been released from prison in 2000. Of these, **45.8%** re-offended within a year and **78.4%** within nine years

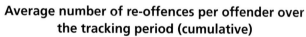

Average number of re-offences per offender over the tracking period (cumulative)

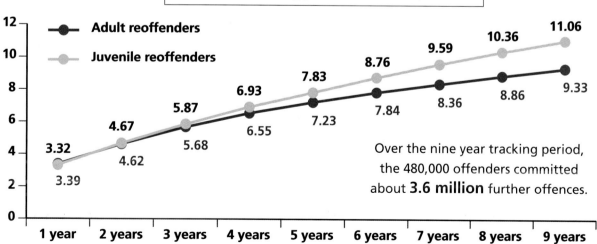

Adult reoffenders

Juvenile reoffenders

	1 year	2 years	3 years	4 years	5 years	6 years	7 years	8 years	9 years
Juvenile	3.39	4.67	5.87	6.93	7.83	8.76	9.59	10.36	11.06
Adult	3.32	4.62	5.68	6.55	7.23	7.84	8.36	8.86	9.33

Over the nine year tracking period, the 480,000 offenders committed about **3.6 million** further offences.

Sources: 2012 Compendium of re-offending statistics & analysis
Ministry of Justice © Crown copyright 2012
www.justice.gov.uk

SEE ALSO:
www.completeissues.co.uk

Crime scene

The Crime Survey for England and Wales tells us about people's experience of crime in the previous 12 months.

9.5 million crimes were reported in the Crime Survey for England and Wales (CSEW), and an estimated **further 1 million** personal crimes against children aged 10 to 15.

CSEW crimes 2011/12, by crime types

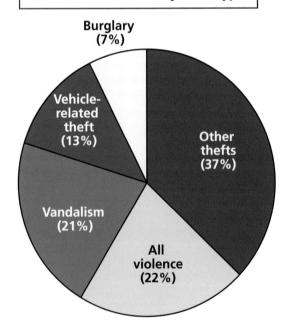

Burglary (7%)

Vehicle-related theft (13%)

Vandalism (21%)

All violence (22%)

Other thefts (37%)

Household crimes
16 in 100 households had been victims

- **2 in 100** households had experienced a burglary (in half of these cases nothing was taken)

- **5 in 100** households owning vehicles had been victims of a vehicle-related theft

- **6 in 100** households had experienced vandalism of household property (eg scratching of car bodywork or breaking a fence or wall)

Personal crimes
6 in 100 adults had been victims

- **1 in 100** adults had been victims of theft from the person (eg pick-pocketing)

- **2 in 100** adults had experienced 'other theft of personal property' (such as unattended bags, wallets, and mobile phones)

- **3 in 100** adults had experienced a violent crime (around a half experiencing violence with injury)

Children aged 10 to 15
experienced higher levels of violence and theft

- **8 in 100** children had been victims of violent crime

- **8 in 100** children had experienced theft while away from the home

Source: Crime Survey for England and Wales - Office for National Statistics, Home Office © Crown copyright 2012
www.ons.gov.uk

SEE ALSO:
www.completeissues.co.uk

Thinner blue line

Police forces are cutting staff, but can they maintain the frontline?

Frontline staff are those who are in everyday contact with the public and who enforce the law: from patrolling neighbourhoods, responding to 999 calls, air support and roads policing to protection of vulnerable people.

Frontline officers also work in less visible ways investigating crime, managing sex offenders and tackling organised crime, for example.

Police Service staff at 31 March, England and Wales

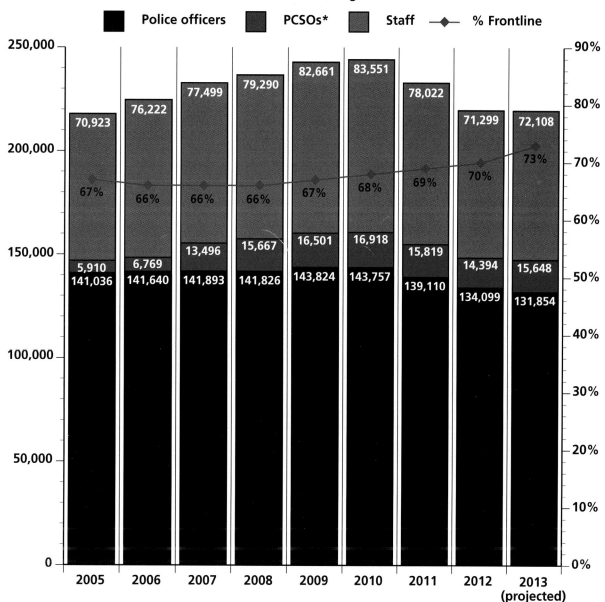

Legend	
■ Police officers	■ PCSOs*
■ Staff	◆ % Frontline

Year	Staff	PCSOs*	Police officers	% Frontline
2005	70,923	5,910	141,036	67%
2006	76,222	6,769	141,640	66%
2007	77,499	13,496	141,893	66%
2008	79,290	15,667	141,826	66%
2009	82,661	16,501	143,824	67%
2010	83,551	16,918	143,757	68%
2011	78,022	15,819	139,110	69%
2012	71,299	14,394	134,099	70%
2013 (projected)	72,108	15,648	131,854	73%

*Police Community Support Officers are members of staff whose role is to support regular police officers and provide a visible uniformed presence in the community

Source: Policing in austerity: One year on, July 2012, HMIC © Crown copyright
www.hmic.gov.uk

SEE ALSO:
www.completeissues.co.uk

If you could see yourself...

... would you see rape?
Sex with someone who doesn't want it IS rape

Get your facts straight

MYTH: ONLY LOUD OR FLIRTATIOUS GIRLS IN TIGHT CLOTHES, OR WEARING SHORT SKIRTS GET RAPED

FACT: Rape is NEVER the victim's fault. People who are assaulted can be of any age, sex, religion, come from any culture or background and be gay, straight or bisexual.

MYTH: A RAPIST IS LIKELY TO BE A STRANGER WHO RAPES SOMEONE IN A DARK ALLEY

FACT: Most rapes are committed by people who know and trust each other. They could be friends, partners, family members or know each other from school, college or work.

MYTH: ALCOHOL AND DRUGS TURN PEOPLE INTO RAPISTS

FACT: Drugs and alcohol are never the cause of rape or sexual assault. It is the attacker who is committing the crime NOT the drugs and/or alcohol.

MYTH: WHEN IT COMES TO SEX GIRLS SAY 'NO' BUT THEY REALLY MEAN 'YES'

FACT: If two people want to have sex with each other it should be something that they BOTH agree and consent to.

MYTH: RAPE IS ONLY RAPE IF SOMEONE GETS PHYSICALLY INJURED

FACT: In some cases people who have been raped have injuries outside or inside their bodies, but not always. Just because someone hasn't got any injuries doesn't mean they weren't raped.

MYTH: IT IS NOT RAPE IF THE VICTIM DOES NOT CLEARLY SAY 'NO'

FACT: Someone doesn't have to say the word NO to withhold permission. There are lots of ways they might say they don't want to have sex. Many people find it hard to say anything, and will show through their body language that they don't want to.

MYTH: RAPE IS ONLY RAPE IF SOMEONE GETS PHYSICALLY FORCED INTO SEX

FACT: Rapists often use emotional pressure and manipulative techniques to intimidate and pressure their victims into sex, rather than physical force.

MYTH: IF TWO PEOPLE HAVE HAD SEX BEFORE, IT'S ALWAYS OK TO HAVE SEX AGAIN

FACT: Just because two people have had sex before it does not mean that consent is not needed the next time they have sex.

MYTH: PEOPLE OFTEN LIE ABOUT BEING RAPED AS THEY REGRET HAVING SEX WITH SOMEONE

FACT: Most people who have been raped or sexually assaulted tell the truth. In fact most people do not tell anyone that they have been raped because they feel too ashamed and scared. Estimates suggest around 8-10% of all rape complaints are false.

A Mumsnet survey of **1,600 women** told of their experiences of rape and sexual assault.

10% had been raped

35% had been sexually assaulted

Of those who had been raped or assaulted

23% had been raped or sexually assaulted **four or more times.**

In **66%** of cases the women knew the person responsible.

Being pressured or forced to have sex when you don't want to is a crime

" She said she didn't want to... I don't think she meant it "

Many women felt unable to report rape or sexual assault

Rape and sexual assaults upon women and girls are far more widespread than official figures show because these offences are under reported.

83% did not report the attacks to the police.

53% said they would be too embarrassed or ashamed to report the crime to the police – they were afraid of being blamed because of their clothes, because they'd drunk alcohol or had stayed with an abusive partner.

68% said they would hesitate to report it to the police mainly because they had little confidence that their attacker would be convicted.

29% didn't tell anyone at all, including friends or family.

The results also revealed that most women felt that rape victims were treated poorly and that the media, **70%**, the legal system, **53%** and society generally, **55%**, were unsympathetic to women who report rape.

Official figures suggest though that police forces have got better at looking after rape victims in recent years shown by a **26%** increase in the number of rapes reported.

http://thisisabuse.direct.gov.uk

Sources: Mumsnet 'We believe you' campaign;
National Community Safety Network
www.mumsnet.com
www.community-safety.net

SEE ALSO:
How my rapist walked free,
Essential Articles 15, p150
www.completeissues.co.uk

Clare's legacy

A tragedy has led to new ways of helping people at risk

The Domestic Violence Disclosure Scheme (DVDS), known as Clare's Law, began to be tried out by Police in Greater Manchester, Gwent, Wiltshire and Nottingham in September 2012.

It offers people a way to find out if someone in a relationship has a violent or abusive past.

It is named after Clare Wood who was murdered in 2009 by her former partner who, unknown to her, had convictions for violence against women.

Although Clare's was an extreme case, the figures show that domestic abuse is not uncommon.

Respondents who had experienced the following, once or more, since the age of 16

(Base: 5,106 people as a sub-sample of the British Crime Survey)

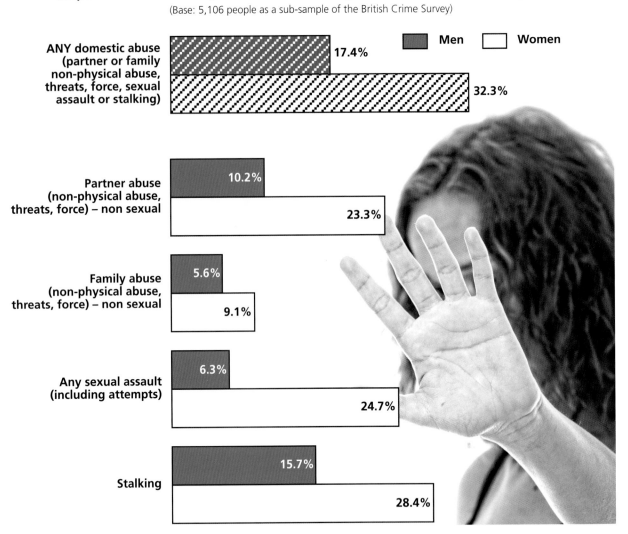

Men   Women

ANY domestic abuse (partner or family non-physical abuse, threats, force, sexual assault or stalking)
17.4%
32.3%

Partner abuse (non-physical abuse, threats, force) – non sexual
10.2%
23.3%

Family abuse (non-physical abuse, threats, force) – non sexual
5.6%
9.1%

Any sexual assault (including attempts)
6.3%
24.7%

Stalking
15.7%
28.4%

A new definition of domestic violence will now include 'coercive control' – patterns of behaviour and separate events that can add up to abuse – intimidation, isolation, depriving victims of their financial independence or material possessions and regulating their everyday behaviour.

The new definition will be implemented by March 2013.

Source: Analysis of the 2010/11 British Crime Survey intimate personal violence split- sample experiment © crown copyright 2012
www.homeoffice.gov
www.endthefear.co.uk

SEE ALSO:
www.completeissues.co.uk

Religion

Religious world

There are 2.18 billion Christians around the world, nearly a third of the global population

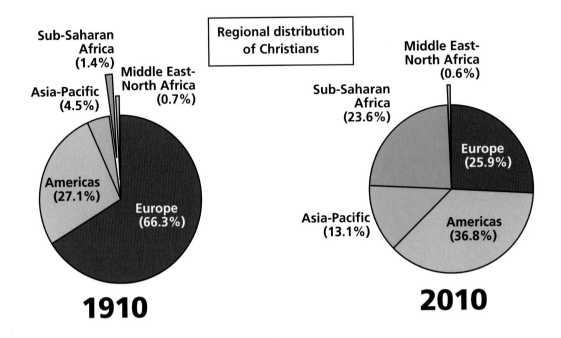

Regional distribution of Christians

1910

Sub-Saharan Africa (1.4%)
Middle East-North Africa (0.7%)
Asia-Pacific (4.5%)
Americas (27.1%)
Europe (66.3%)

2010

Middle East-North Africa (0.6%)
Sub-Saharan Africa (23.6%)
Europe (25.9%)
Asia-Pacific (13.1%)
Americas (36.8%)

The Christian proportion of the world population has fallen very slightly from **35%** in 1910 to **32%**.

One area of enormous growth has been sub-Saharan Africa where the proportion of Christians in the population has risen from **9%** to **63%**.

10 Countries with the largest number of Christians	Estimated 2010 Christian population	% of population that is Christian	% of world Christian population
United States	246,780,000	79.5	11.3
Brazil	175,770,000	90.2	8.0
Mexico	107,780,000	95.0	4.9
Russia	105,220,000	73.6	4.8
Philippines	86,790,000	93.1	4.0
Nigeria	80,510,000	50.8	3.7
China	67,070,000	5.0	3.1
DR Congo	63,150,000	95.7	2.9
Germany	58,240,000	70.8	2.7
Ethiopia	52,580,000	63.4	2.4
Subtotal for the 10 Countries	1,043,880,000	40.4	47.8
Total for Rest of World	1,140,180,000	6.3	52.2
World Total	2,184,060,000	31.7	100.0

Major Christian Traditions
% of the Christian population that is:

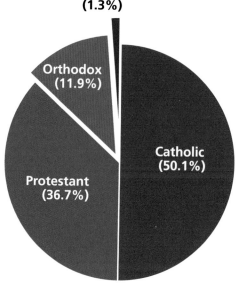

Other Christian (1.3%)

Orthodox (11.9%)

Protestant (36.7%)

Catholic (50.1%)

Within the world's Christians there are differences in the way they practise their religion and in the details of beliefs.

Estimated size of Christian Traditions

Countries	Estimated 2010 Christian population	% of world population	% of world Christian population
Catholic	1,094,610,000	15.9	50.1
Protestant	800,640,000	11.6	36.7
Orthodox	260,380,000	3.8	11.9
Other* Christian	28,430,000	0.4	1.3
Total Christian	2,184,060,000	31.7	100.0

*Other includes the Church of Jesus Christ of the Latter Day Saints (Mormons), Jehovah's Witnesses and the Christian Science Church

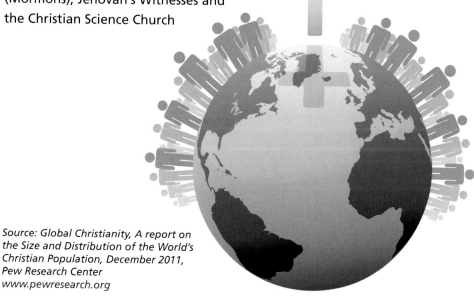

Source: Global Christianity, A report on the Size and Distribution of the World's Christian Population, December 2011, Pew Research Center
www.pewresearch.org

SEE ALSO:
www.completeissues.co.uk

Practising Christians?

How religious are UK Christians?

A representative sample of 2,107 adults aged 15+ across the UK were surveyed in the week after the 2011 Census.

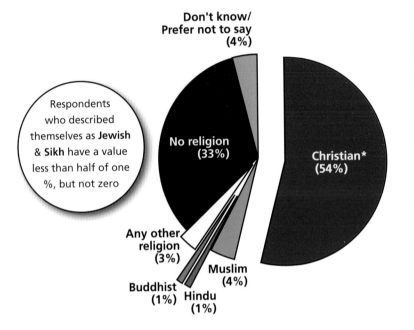

The religion respondents recorded (or would have recorded) on the 2011 Census

Don't know/ Prefer not to say (4%)

Respondents who described themselves as **Jewish** & **Sikh** have a value less than half of one %, but not zero

No religion (33%)

Christian* (54%)

Any other religion (3%)

Buddhist (1%)

Hindu (1%)

Muslim (4%)

The number of UK adults who identify themselves as Christian has fallen significantly since 2001.

72%

said they were Christian in the 2001 Census.

The MAIN reason respondents thought of themselves as being Christian

(1,136 adults defined themselves as Christian in 2011)

46%
were christened/baptised into this religion

8%
went to a Christian Sunday school as a child

4%
went to a Christian school

18%
believed in the teachings of Christianity

4%
CURRENTLY attended religious services at church other than weddings, christenings/ baptisms or funerals and

3%
USED TO attend

13%
said one or both of their parents are/were Christians

1%
said their husband/wife/ partner is/was a member of this religion and

1%
said their child/children attend/s a Christian school

3%
Didn't know/ preferred not to say

* Christian includes Church of England, Catholic, Protestant and all other Christian denominations

Church attendance

The low level of religious belief and practice among those calling themselves Christian is reflected in church attendance.

Apart from special occasions such as weddings, funerals and baptisms:

49%
had not attended a church service in the previous 12 months.

16%
hadn't attended for **more than 10 years** and

12%
have **never** attended.

45%
of respondents considered themselves to be religious

37%
of respondents had **NEVER** or **almost never** prayed except in a church service

Religious activity

When asked whether in the last 12 months they had chosen to take part in a non-church-based religious activity eg watching or listening to a religious service on the TV, radio or internet

53%
hadn't taken part at all

The Bible

15%
admitted to having **never** read the Bible except in a church service

36%
hadn't done so in the previous **three years**

60%
hadn't read any part of the Bible out of choice, for **at least a year**

64%
were **NOT** able to identify Matthew as the first book of the New Testament

Source: Ipsos MORI Poll for Richard Dawkins Foundation for Reason and Science (UK) – How religious are UK Christians?
www.richarddawkins.net
www.ipsos-mori.com

SEE ALSO:
www.completeissues.co.uk

Believe it ... or not

Younger people are more likely to have no religious belief

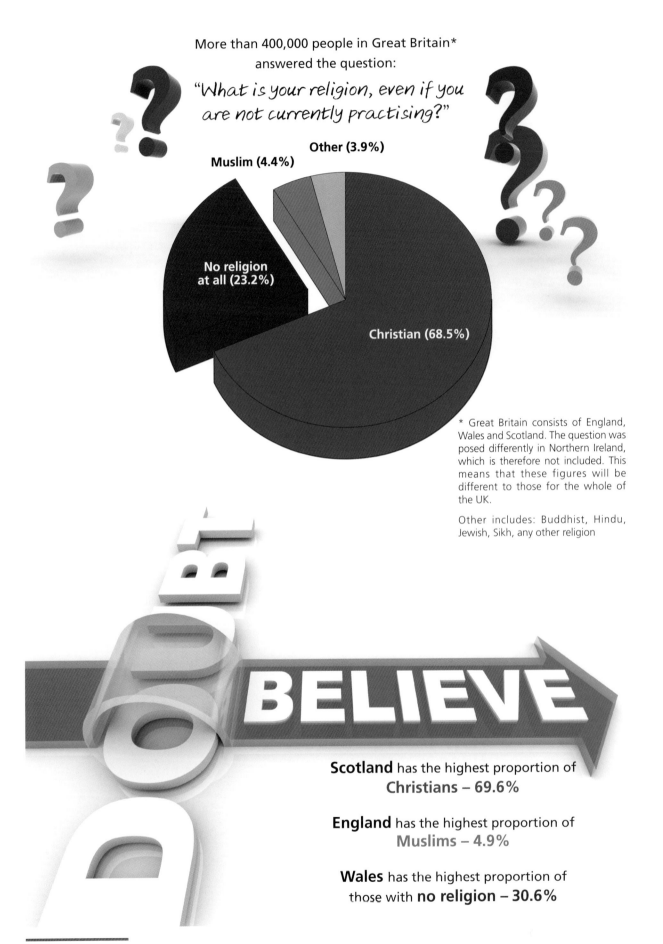

More than 400,000 people in Great Britain*
answered the question:

*"What is your religion, even if you
are not currently practising?"*

Other (3.9%)

Muslim (4.4%)

No religion
at all (23.2%)

Christian (68.5%)

* Great Britain consists of England,
Wales and Scotland. The question was
posed differently in Northern Ireland,
which is therefore not included. This
means that these figures will be
different to those for the whole of
the UK.

Other includes: Buddhist, Hindu,
Jewish, Sikh, any other religion

Scotland has the highest proportion of
Christians – 69.6%

England has the highest proportion of
Muslims – 4.9%

Wales has the highest proportion of
those with **no religion – 30.6%**

Religious commitment varies between age groups

Those *aged 25-34* are most likely to have **no religion**
while **92%** in the *65+ age group* identify with a religion

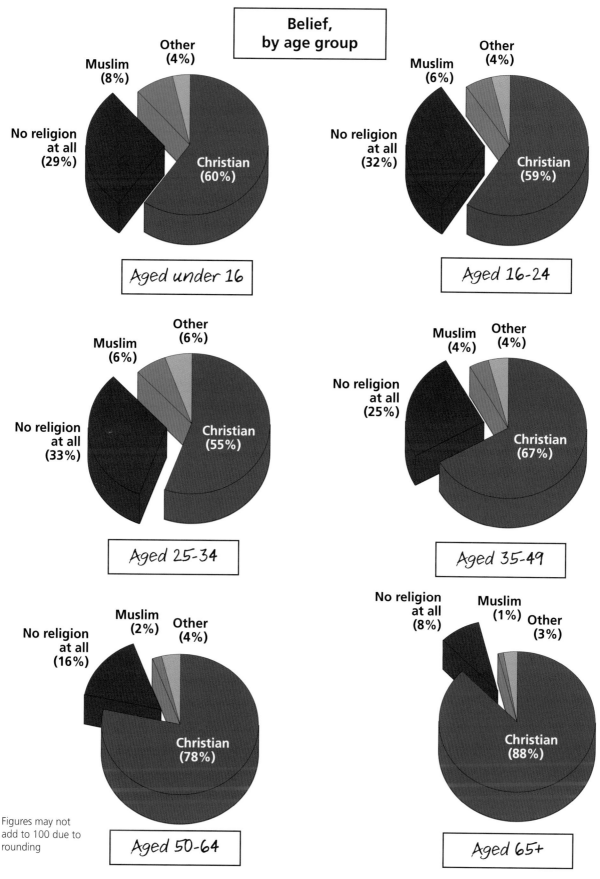

Belief,
by age group

Aged under 16
- Other (4%)
- Muslim (8%)
- No religion at all (29%)
- Christian (60%)

Aged 16-24
- Other (4%)
- Muslim (6%)
- No religion at all (32%)
- Christian (59%)

Aged 25-34
- Other (6%)
- Muslim (6%)
- No religion at all (33%)
- Christian (55%)

Aged 35-49
- Muslim (4%)
- Other (4%)
- No religion at all (25%)
- Christian (67%)

Aged 50-64
- Muslim (2%)
- Other (4%)
- No religion at all (16%)
- Christian (78%)

Aged 65+
- No religion at all (8%)
- Muslim (1%)
- Other (3%)
- Christian (88%)

Figures may not add to 100 due to rounding

Source Integrated Household Survey Experimental Statistics, September 2011 – Office for National Statistics © Crown copyright 2012
www.ons.gov.uk

SEE ALSO:
www.completeissues.co.uk

I believe...

Many people who say they are Christian hold beliefs that do not fit traditional Christian teaching

Q **Which of the following statements comes closest to describing you?**

(Base: 1,136 adults aged 15+ across the UK who referred to themselves as Christian)

30% said I HAVE strong religious beliefs and I AM A CHRISTIAN

29% said I DO NOT have strong religious beliefs but I THINK OF MYSELF AS A CHRISTIAN

19% said I DO NOT have strong religious beliefs but I was BROUGHT UP to think of myself as a Christian

12% said I WOULDN'T REALLY CALL MYSELF RELIGIOUS at all

8% said I think of myself as being SPIRITUAL RATHER THAN RELIGIOUS

2% said Don't know or preferred not to say

1% said None of these

Q **Which of the following statements best describes your personal view of God?**

(Base: 1,136 adults aged 15+ across the UK who referred to themselves as Christian)

37% said I BELIEVE IN GOD and I believe that Christianity is just ONE WAY of knowing him

17% said I BELIEVE IN GOD and I believe that Christianity is the ONLY TRUE WAY of knowing him

13% said I think of God as being the LAWS OF NATURE and everything in the universe

10% said I DON'T BELIEVE in God but think there may be some kind of supernatural intelligence out there

9% said I think of God as being whatever CAUSED THE UNIVERSE

6% said Don't know or preferred not to say

1% said None of these

6% said I DON'T BELIEVE IN GOD

NB Results may not add up to 100% due to rounding

Many who say they are Christian hold beliefs that some churches would consider not to fit with traditional Christian teaching, such as astrology and reincarnation, ghosts and fate

Q **To what extent do you personally believe in the following?**
(Base: 1,136 adults aged 15+ across the UK who referred to themselves as Christian)

- Completely/To some extent
- Not sure
- Not really/Not at all
- Don't know/Prefer not to say

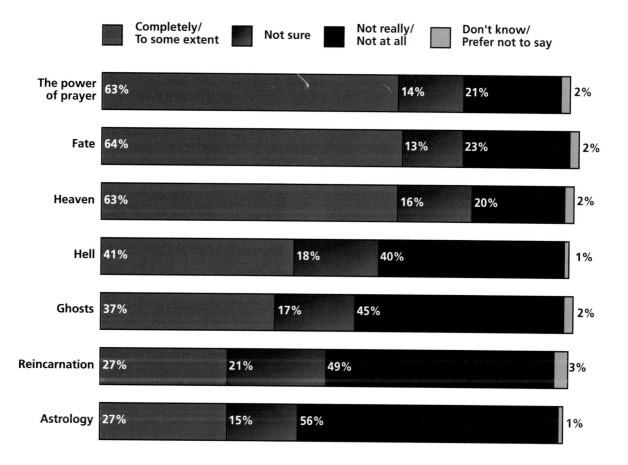

	Completely/To some extent	Not sure	Not really/Not at all	Don't know/Prefer not to say
The power of prayer	63%	14%	21%	2%
Fate	64%	13%	23%	2%
Heaven	63%	16%	20%	2%
Hell	41%	18%	40%	1%
Ghosts	37%	17%	45%	2%
Reincarnation	27%	21%	49%	3%
Astrology	27%	15%	56%	1%

Source: Ipsos MORI Poll for Richard Dawkins Foundation for Reason and Science (UK) – How religious are UK Christians?
www.richarddawkins.net
www.ipsos-mori.com

SEE ALSO:
www.completeissues.co.uk

Do you feel lucky?

Have superstitions lasted because they can come true?
A surprising number of people think they can!

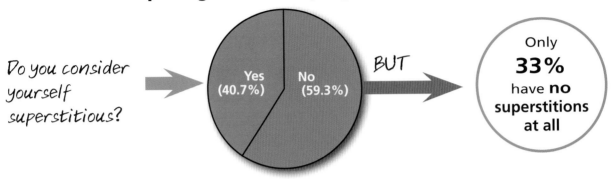

Do you consider yourself superstitious?

Yes (40.7%) | **No (59.3%)**

BUT

Only **33%** have **no** superstitions at all

Which of these superstitions do you stick to?

Superstition	Percentage
Not walking underneath a ladder	38.2%
Touching wood to avoid tempting fate	33.3%
Not opening umbrellas indoors	26.6%
Crossing your fingers for good luck	26.3%
Not putting new shoes on the table	23.5%
Picking up a penny from the floor for good luck	20.0%
Throwing spilt salt over your shoulder	19.1%
Not passing anyone on the stairs	12.5%
Not walking on cracks in the pavement	10.8%
Carry a lucky charm	4.9%
Getting out of bed on the same side you got in to avoid bad luck	3.6%
Hang horseshoe over the fireplace/door	2.4%
Other	1.4%

When asked:

"Have you ever seen a superstition come true? eg breaking a mirror did bring bad luck"

54% answered No, never and **19%** couldn't remember

but a total of **15%** think superstitions come true sometimes

12% said everytime or almost everytime

OnePoll draws a sample of at least 1,000 from a panel of over 100,000 members of all ages, income groups, attitudes and behaviours

Source; OnePoll Data Hub
news.onepoll.com

SEE ALSO:
www.completeissues.co.uk

Sport

Who won?

Official Olympic medal rankings tell us who won most gold medals – but there are other ways of looking at the achievements

Top ten Olympic medal winning countries, official ranking by gold medals won, 2012

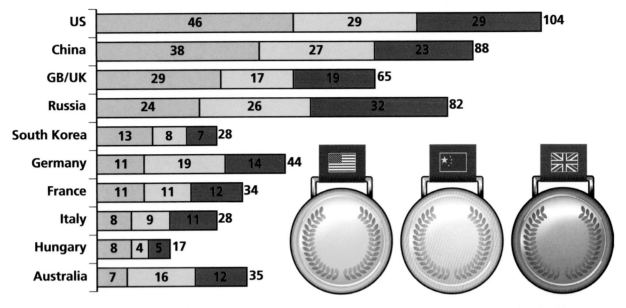

Country	Gold	Silver	Bronze	Total
US	46	29	29	104
China	38	27	23	88
GB/UK	29	17	19	65
Russia	24	26	32	82
South Korea	13	8	7	28
Germany	11	19	14	44
France	11	11	12	34
Italy	8	9	11	28
Hungary	8	4	5	17
Australia	7	16	12	35

Some countries have much **bigger populations** than others – so they should have the advantage of a **bigger pool of talented athletes**. If the rankings were re-calculated to take account of population size:

	Ranking by Population	Official ranking by gold medal	Total number of medals won
1	Grenada	50	1
2	Jamaica	18	12
3	Bahamas	50	1
4	New Zealand	15	13
5	Trinidad &Tobago	47	4
6	Montenegro	69	1
7	Cyprus	69	1
8	Hungary	9	17
9	Slovenia	42	4
10	Denmark	29	9
11	GB/UK	3	65

Some countries are much **wealthier** than others – so they should have the advantage of **more resources**. If the rankings were re-calculated to take account of GDP*:

	Ranking by GDP	Official ranking by gold medal	Total number of medals won
1	Grenada	50	1
2	Jamaica	18	12
3	North Korea	20	6
4	Mongolia	56	5
5	Georgia	39	7
6	Kenya	28	11
7	Montenegro	69	1
8	Belarus	26	12
9	Armenia	60	3
10	Ethiopia	24	7
40	GB/UK	3	65

*Gross Domestic Product is the market value of all officially recognised final goods and services produced within a country in a given period of time. GDP per head is a useful indicator of a country's standard of living

Britain came third in the medal table. How much did British success cost?

Number of medals won respectively gold, silver, bronze

Sport	Cost	Gold	Silver	Bronze
Boxing	£1,910,280	3	1	1
Cycling	£2,169,333	8	2	2
Taekwondo	£2,416,800	1		1
Shooting	£2,461,866	1		
Triathlon	£2,645,650	1		1
Equestrian	£2,679,020	3	1	1
Gymnastics	£2,692,650		1	3
Rowing	£3,031,956	4	2	3
Judo	£3,749,000		1	1
Canoeing	£4,044,175	2	1	1
Athletics	£4,191,333	4	1	1
Sailing	£4,588,540	1	4	
Modern Pentathlon	£6,288,800		1	
Diving	£6,535,700			1
Swimming	£8,381,533		1	2
Hockey	£15,013,200			1

Average cost of a medal £4,192,758

The amount of money invested in each Olympic sport by UKSport since the 2008 Beijing Olympics was divided by the number of medals won in each sport.

Olympic sports which were supported by UK Sport but which did not win any medals were:

Sport	Cost	Sport	Cost
Archery	£4,408,000	Table Tennis	£1,213,848
Badminton	£7,434,900	Volleyball	£3,536,077
Basketball	£8,599,000	Water Polo	£2,928,039
Fencing	£2,529,335	Weightlifting	£1,365,157
Handball	£2,924,721	Wrestling	£1,435,210
Synchronised Swimming	£3,398,300		

Total UK Sport spending on Olympic sports:

£264,143,753

Total medals won 63
Average cost per medal:

£4,192,758

PA Wire/Press Association Images

Source: The Guardian, London 2012
www.guardian.co.uk/data
www.london2012.com

SEE ALSO:
No parallel, p154-155
www.completeissues.co.uk

No parallel

The Paralympic games were a huge success in promoting sport and changing attitudes

In the first games to be known as Paralympics (Rome 1960), 400 athletes from 21 nations took part in nine events. In 2012, more than 4,000 competed in 20 sports.

In Rio in 2016 Para-Canoe and Para-Triathlon will make their debuts taking the total of sports to 22.

Paralympics 2012, official ranking by gold medals won, top ten countries

Rank by gold	Country	Gold	Silver	Bronze
1	People's Republic of China	95	71	65
2	Russian Federation	36	38	28
3	Great Britain	34	43	43
4	Ukraine	32	24	28
5	Australia	32	23	30
6	United States of America	31	29	38
7	Brazil	21	14	8
8	Germany	18	26	22
9	Poland	14	13	9
10	Netherlands	10	10	19

565 records were broken at the Paralympic games: **333 Paralympic** records and **232 world** records

Great Britain won a total of **120 medals – 39** of these were in **swimming, 29** in **athletics, 22** in **cycling** (7 road, 15 track) and **11** in **equestrian**.

Sarah Storey and **David Weir** were the most decorated British athletes with **four gold medals**.

Sarah Storey also set a Paralympic and world record.

Great Britain's David Weir (centre) celebrating after winning gold in the Men's 800m – T54, during the Paralympic Games in London on 6th September 2012

Photo: Anthony Devlin, PA Wire/Press Association Images

The Games were a huge success with the public

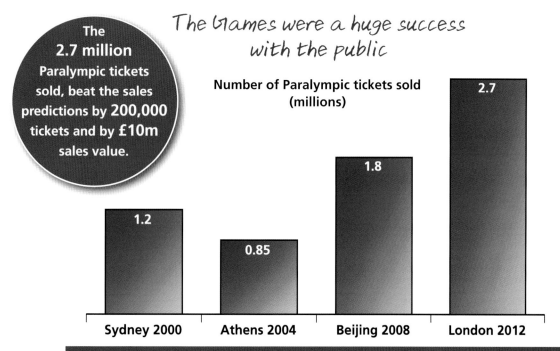

The **2.7 million** Paralympic tickets sold, beat the sales predictions by **200,000** tickets and by **£10m** sales value.

Number of Paralympic tickets sold (millions)

- Sydney 2000: 1.2
- Athens 2004: 0.85
- Beijing 2008: 1.8
- London 2012: 2.7

Channel 4, which broadcast the Paralympics, saw its share of the time people spent watching TV rise from **one hour 17 minutes per person** (5%) in the week before the games to **two hours 44 minutes** (10%) during them. The share fell to **one hour 25 minutes** after the games had finished.

Even before the opening ceremony, attitudes were changing and the Games changed them still more

The Paralympic Games are making me feel more positive about the role of people with disabilities in UK society.

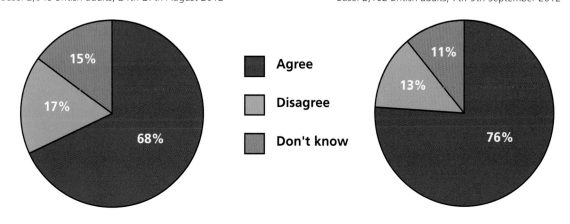

Before the Paralympics
Base: 2,045 British adults, 24th-27th August 2012

- Agree: 68%
- Disagree: 17%
- Don't know: 15%

During/After the Paralympics
Base: 2,102 British adults, 7th-9th September 2012

- Agree: 76%
- Disagree: 13%
- Don't know: 11%

I think that the perception of disability has changed. People are now looking at ability not disability. It has left a legacy.

Natasha Baker (Equestrian)

Sources: Paralympics Surveys, ComRes; London 2012; BARB
www.comres.co.uk
www.london2012.com/paralympics
www.barb.co.uk

SEE ALSO:
Who won?, p152-153
www.completeissues.co.uk

Games for girls

What is stopping girls getting enough exercise?

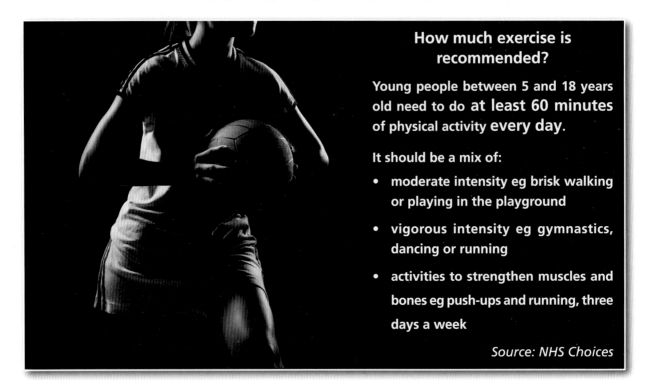

How much exercise is recommended?

Young people between 5 and 18 years old need to do **at least 60 minutes** of physical activity **every day**.

It should be a mix of:

- moderate intensity eg brisk walking or playing in the playground
- vigorous intensity eg gymnastics, dancing or running
- activities to strengthen muscles and bones eg push-ups and running, three days a week

Source: NHS Choices

Official figures show that just **12%** of 14-year-old girls are reaching the recommended levels of physical activity – **half** the number of boys at the same age... but **74%** of girls say they would **like to be more active**.

1,500 school children were questioned in a survey about their attitudes to fitness and sport.

51% of girls are put off physical activity because of their experiences of school sport and PE

School

46% of the **least active** girls say they don't like the activities they get to do in PE. Only **26%** of the **most active** girls feel this way

Competitive

45% of girls say sport is too competitive

More than half think boys enjoy competitive sport more than girls

Friends

57% of all girls agreed that girls drop out of sport and other physical activity because their friends do

Role models

43% of girls agree that there aren't many sporting role models for girls

" ...school sport plays a key role in shaping attitudes to health and fitness. "
Sue Tibballs,
Chief Executive, Women's Sport and Fitness Foundation (WSFF)

Body image

76% of all girls agree that girls are self-conscious about their bodies

Just over a quarter of girls agree that they feel their body is on show in PE and this makes them like PE less

Feminine?

48% of girls surveyed say that getting sweaty is not feminine

Nearly a third of boys think that girls who are sporty are not very feminine

Opportunity

Over half of all boys and girls agree that there are more opportunities for boys to succeed in sport than girls

A large number feel that too much PE and school sport is still focused on traditional competitive sport, and attention reserved for the sporty and talented

What do girls want?

- a greater choice of activities;
- girl-only groups;
- to be with their friends and have fun while exercising;
- to feel comfortable in what they wear; and
- to feel encouraged and rewarded for their efforts.

- Physical inactivity among children can lead to obesity and low self-esteem.
- Physical health affects children's ability to learn.
- Taking part in sport and exercise develops skills in organisation, teamwork and leadership.
- For girls particularly, being physically active helps to develop a positive body image – crucial when **30%** of girls aged 11-16 say they lack confidence in their appearance.

Gender gap

Girls become less positive about sport and physical activity as they get older. In Year 4 of primary school, girls and boys are doing similar levels of physical activity.

By Year 6, girls are doing considerably less exercise than boys and the gap widens as girls reach Year 9 of secondary school.

Source: Changing the game for girls – Women's Sport and Fitness Foundation (WSFF); Institute of Youth Sport at Loughborough University; NHS Choices
www.wsff.org.uk
www.lboro.ac.uk
www.nhs.uk

SEE ALSO:
www.completeissues.co.uk

(Un)fit Britain?

35% of Brits say they exercise less than once a week

It is recommended that adults need to do two and half hours each week of moderate to vigorous intensity physical activity such as cycling or fast walking – and aim to do some physical activity every day. Muscle strengthening should also be included twice a week.

% who exercise less than once a week, 2011
Base: 2,017 UK adults aged 18+

In Scotland and Northern Ireland, only 18% of people exercise more than 3 times a week

24% of UK adults exercise more than 3 times a week

27% exercise 2-3 times a week

14% exercise once a week

Scotland 43%

Northern Ireland 38%

North East 34%

Yorkshire & Humberside 38%

North West 45%

East Midlands 35%

Wales 30%

East of England 36%

West Midlands 32%

London 30%

South East 32%

South West 32%

The South West has the highest percentage saying they exercise more than 3 times a week – 29% – followed by London – 27%

London and Wales are the most exercise-happy regions in the UK with 70% in each saying they exercise at least once a week

Source: Opinium Research, Department of Health © Crown copyright 2012
www.opinium.co.uk
www.dh.gov.uk

SEE ALSO:
www.completeissues.co.uk

War & conflict

Showing support

UK support for the military is very high – but they show it more in the US

2,033 UK adults along with 2,048 US adults were interviewed as part of the biggest ever research project among military personnel and the general public.

2,033 UK adults were asked how positive or negative their view of each of the following were on a scale of 0 to 10, where 0 meant very negative and 10 meant very positive

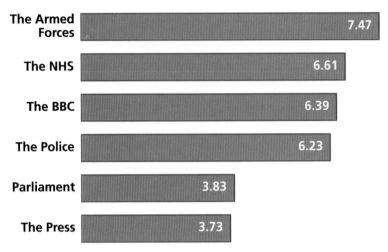

The Armed Forces	7.47
The NHS	6.61
The BBC	6.39
The Police	6.23
Parliament	3.83
The Press	3.73

Those that gave a high score (6-10) in their view of the Armed Forces, were asked their reasons
(Base: 1,065 who gave a high score)

45% said: "They do a great/ important job/ I wouldn't want to do it"

21% said: "Personnel risk their lives"

11% said: "Brave/courageous/ heroes/decent/ selfless"

Although support for troops is high, there is a difference between how people in the UK and the US demonstrate this

When you see, or if you saw, a member of the Armed Forces out and about in uniform in a town, have you ever, or could you see yourself going up to thank them for their service?

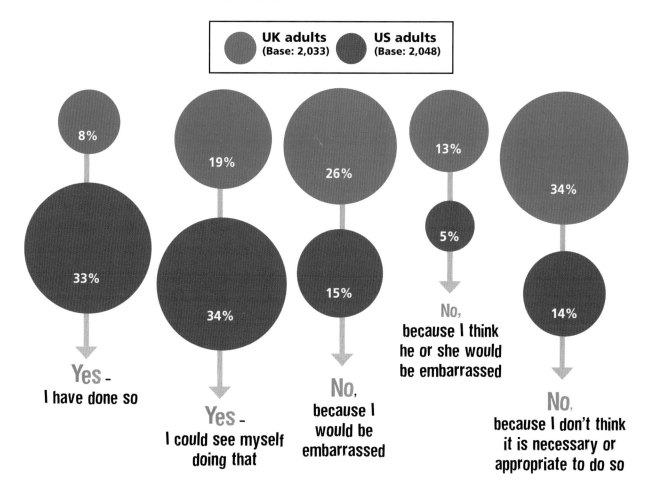

UK adults (Base: 2,033)
US adults (Base: 2,048)

8%
19%
26%
13%
34%

33%
34%
15%
5%
14%

Yes - I have done so

Yes - I could see myself doing that

No, because I would be embarrassed

No, because I think he or she would be embarrassed

No, because I don't think it is necessary or appropriate to do so

Quotes from respondents in British Army focus group

"A lot of people come over and just very quietly say, 'Are you in the Army?' and they just shake your hand."

"The Americans have got it right. They're less cynical people. They genuinely believe their armed forces are the first and last line of defence for their country. Patriotism plays a massive part, whereas I don't think it plays any part, really, in British cultural life."

"With regard to the amount of public reaction we get in the UK, I feel quite happy with it, it's appropriate. If we were to compare it with the US, I wouldn't want to be on some kind of pedestal. I think British society holds us in esteem, and I think it's appropriate."

"I stopped off in an airport in America and there was a massive flag and loads of posters saying 'Welcome home troops'. I thought, bloody hell, you don't get that in Manchester Airport."

Source: Lord Ashcroft Polls © Lord Ashcroft May 2012; The Armed Forces & Society www.lordashcroftpolls.com

SEE ALSO:
Feeling supported, p162-163
www.completeissues.co.uk

Feeling supported

92% of service personnel thought the general public had a positive view about the Forces

9,106 UK Service personnel were interviewed as part of the biggest ever research project among military personnel and the general public.

Those who had served longest often said public support for the Forces was **higher** than they'd ever known it.

Those in more senior ranks thought this could be due to being **more in the public eye** in recent years, so support could **begin to decrease** after current missions end.

85% of those who had served for more than 20 years said the relationship had improved.

% of Service Personnel who thought the relationship between the Armed Forces and the general public...

...has got better over PAST 5 years — **75%**

...will get better in NEXT five years — **28%**

"At the end of the day, they're paying you for what you've done... for the service you give them. Every taxpayer. So I don't think they need to thank anyone, really".

Respondent in former personnel focus group

Which of the following do you think best describes the way the public feel towards Service personnel?
(More than one answer could be given)

Positive views

- **Supportive** 64%
- **Proud** 51%
- **Respectful** 47%
- **Sympathetic** 34%
- **Grateful** 27%
- **Admiring** 25%

- **Indifferent** 15%

Negative views

- **Wary** 13%
- **Intimidated** 8%
- **Condescending** 5%
- **Jealous** 3%
- **Afraid** 2%

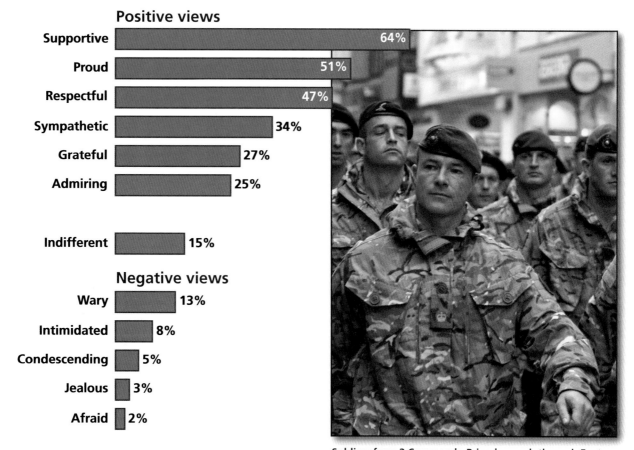

Soldiers from 3 Commando Brigade march through Exeter city centre during the homecoming parade
Photo: Clive Chilvers / Shutterstock.com

% of Service personnel who agreed with the following statements:

- Charities, for example Help for Heroes, are having a positive impact on public perceptions of the Forces — **95%**
- The public support the Armed Forces, even if they don't agree with the operations they are sent on — **80%**
- Recent "fly on the wall" documentaries are having a positive impact on what the public think of the Forces — **80%**
- It is clear that the public are grateful for the military's role in keeping the country safe — **72%**
- Criticism of the Forces by the media is usually unfair, and based on exaggeration or false stories — **68%**

*Source: Lord Ashcroft Polls © Lord Ashcroft May 2012;
The Armed Forces & Society
www.lordashcroftpolls.com*

SEE ALSO:
Showing support, p160-161
www.completeissues.co.uk

Mounting toll

A tally of deaths among those serving in Afghanistan – already the numbers will have risen

Coalition military fatalities in Afghanistan, by year

US UK Other

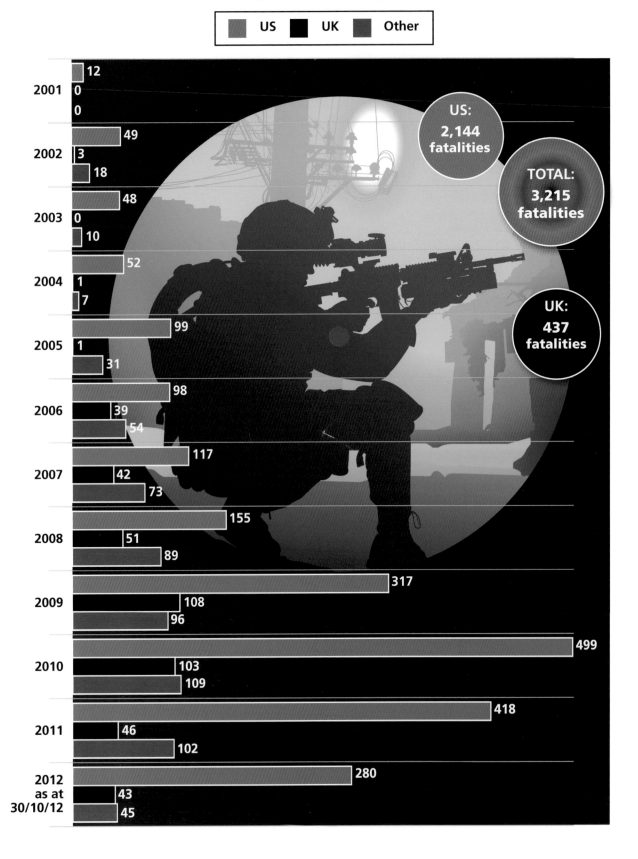

2001
12
0
0

2002
49
3
18

2003
48
0
10

2004
52
1
7

2005
99
1
31

2006
98
39
54

2007
117
42
73

2008
155
51
89

2009
317
108
96

2010
499
103
109

2011
418
46
102

2012
as at
30/10/12
280
43
45

US:
2,144
fatalities

TOTAL:
3,215
fatalities

UK:
437
fatalities

'Other' countries sustaining troop fatalities in Afghanistan, by year

	2001	2002	2003	2004	2005	2006	2007	2008	2009	2010	2011	2012	Totals
Australia	0	1	0	0	0	0	3	3	4	10	11	7	39
Canada	0	4	2	1	1	36	30	32	32	16	4	0	158
Denmark	0	3	0	1	0	0	6	13	7	9	3	0	42
France	0	0	0	3	2	6	3	11	11	16	26	8	86
Germany	0	10	6	0	4	0	7	3	7	9	7	0	53
Italy	0	0	0	1	2	6	2	2	9	12	8	5	47
Netherlands	0	0	0	0	0	4	8	6	3	4	0	0	25
Poland	0	0	0	0	0	0	1	7	8	6	13	0	35
Spain	0	0	0	0	18	1	4	2	1	4	4	0	34

Albania, Belgium, Czech Republic, Estonia, Finland, Georgia, Hungary, Jordan, Latvia, Lithuania, NATO, New Zealand, Norway, Romania, Portugal, South Korea, Sweden and Turkey have also sustained troop fatalities in Afghanistan, totalling a further **115**.

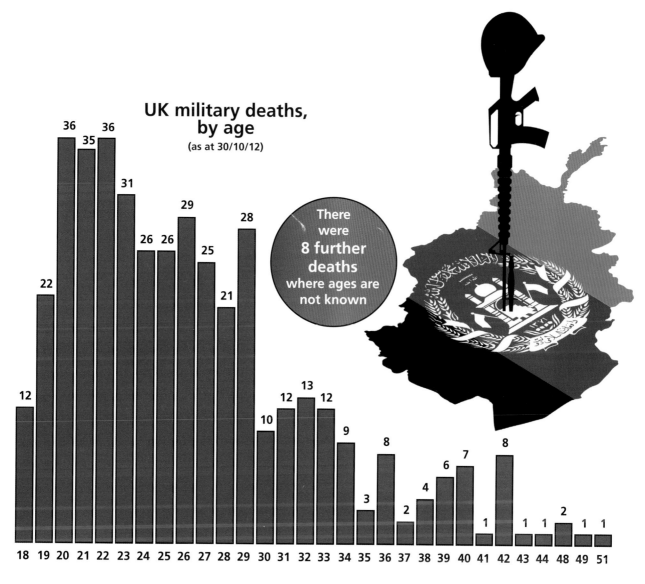

UK military deaths, by age
(as at 30/10/12)

There were **8 further deaths** where ages are not known

Values by age:
18: 12, 19: 22, 20: 36, 21: 35, 22: 36, 23: 31, 24: 26, 25: 26, 26: 29, 27: 25, 28: 21, 29: 28, 30: 10, 31: 12, 32: 13, 33: 12, 34: 9, 35: 3, 36: 8, 37: 2, 38: 4, 39: 6, 40: 7, 41: 1, 42: 8, 43: 1, 44: 1, 48: 2, 49: 1, 51: 1

Source: Operation Enduring Freedom, icasualties.org;
www.icasualties.org

SEE ALSO:
Mother's Day: My grief at the loss of my soldier son in Afghanistan, Essential Articles 15 p182
www.completeissues.co.uk

Caught in the cross-fire

2011 marked the fifth year in a row that civilian casualties increased in the armed conflict in Afghanistan

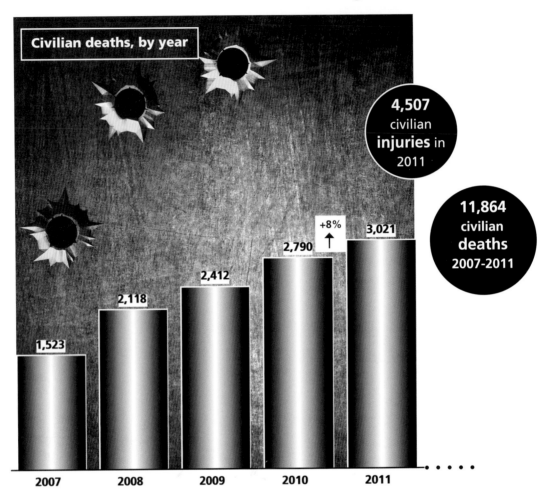

Civilian deaths, by year

4,507 civilian **injuries** in 2011

11,864 civilian **deaths** 2007-2011

1,523 — 2007

2,118 — 2008

2,412 — 2009

2,790 — 2010

+8% ↑

3,021 — 2011

AGEs and PGFs are the groups responsible for the most civilian deaths in Afghanistan.

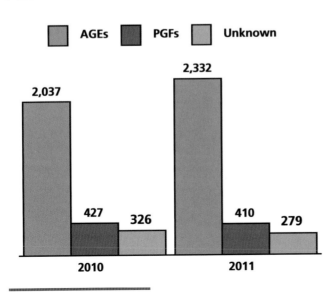

Groups responsible for the civilian deaths 2010-2011

AGEs   PGFs   Unknown

2,037   427   326 — 2010

2,332   410   279 — 2011

AGEs – Anti-Government Elements – individuals or groups eg Taliban, involved in armed conflict against the Government of Afghanistan and/or international military forces.

This group caused the most Afghan civilian deaths in 2011 – **2,332** deaths, amounting to **77%** of all civilians who died in the conflict – this was **up 14%** from 2010.

PGFs – Pro-Government Forces are international military forces, other government agencies such as CIA and Afghan government forces.

This group were responsible for **14%** of all conflict-related civilian deaths - **410** deaths, down 4% from 2010.

9% of deaths **(279)** could not be attributed to a particular group.

The record loss of Afghan civilian lives was mainly due to changes in the tactics of **AGE**s. They used **Improvised Explosive Devices – IED**s – more often and more widely across the country. They carried out deadlier **suicide attacks** causing a greater numbers of victims and increased the unlawful and **targeted killing** of civilians.

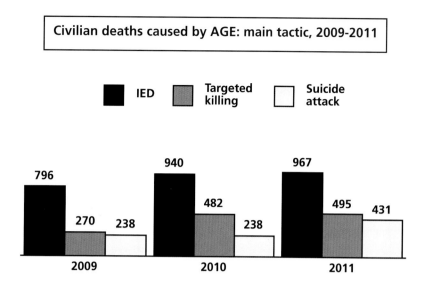

Civilian deaths caused by AGE: main tactic, 2009-2011

■ IED   ▨ Targeted killing   □ Suicide attack

	2009	2010	2011
IED	796	940	967
Targeted killing	270	482	495
Suicide attack	238	238	431

The impact on children

Afghan children play on a military tank

Photo: Lizette Potgieter / Shutterstock.com

82% of children injured or killed were **boys** – they were **four times** more likely to be injured or killed than girls. **Boys** between the ages of **8 to 15** were the most vulnerable group, making up **more than half** of all deaths and injuries.

30% of accidents which claimed a child victim happened while they were **playing**, **15%** happened while **tending to animals** and **12%** happened while **collecting firewood**.

25 of the victims were **under 6**, including three babies.

Source: Protection of Civilians in Armed Conflict Report 2011 – The United Nations Assistance Mission in Afghanistan – UNAMA
http://unama.unmissions.org

SEE ALSO:
www.completeissues.co.uk

Blow the budget

World military spending in 2011 was around US$1.74 trillion

Military expenditure is the money a country spends on all military purposes.

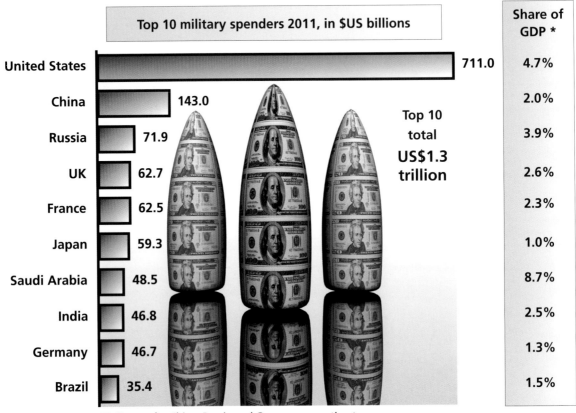

Top 10 military spenders 2011, in $US billions		Share of GDP *
United States	711.0	4.7%
China	143.0	2.0%
Russia	71.9	3.9%
UK	62.7	2.6%
France	62.5	2.3%
Japan	59.3	1.0%
Saudi Arabia	48.5	8.7%
India	46.8	2.5%
Germany	46.7	1.3%
Brazil	35.4	1.5%

Top 10 total US$1.3 trillion

NB Figures for China, Russia and Germany are estimates
*Gross Domestic Product is the market value of all officially recognised final goods and services produced within a country in a given period of time. GDP per head is a useful indicator of a country's standard of living

World share of military expenditure, 2011
Top 10 compared to the rest of the world

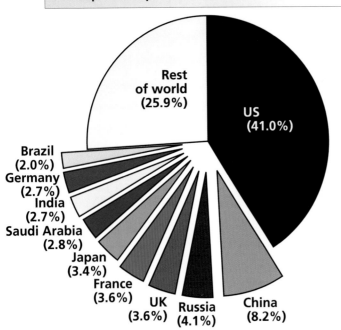

Rest of world (25.9%)
US (41.0%)
Brazil (2.0%)
Germany (2.7%)
India (2.7%)
Saudi Arabia (2.8%)
Japan (3.4%)
France (3.6%)
UK (3.6%)
Russia (4.1%)
China (8.2%)

Six of the world's top military spenders – **Brazil, France, Germany, India, UK and the United States** – **made cuts** in their military budgets in 2011.

Russia in contrast, increased its military spending by **9.3%**, as did **China,** which increased its spend by **$8.2 billion**.

It is expected that the withdrawal from Iraq and the draw-down in Afghanistan will lead to falls in additional war spending in the United States.

SEE ALSO:
What we could do with money wasted on Afghanistan war, Essential Articles 15, p180
www.completeissues.co.uk

Source: © Stockholm International Peace Research Institute (SIPRI)
www.sipri.org

Wider world

Amber planet

Of the nine countries closest to achieving happy, green lives, eight are in Latin America and the Caribbean.

"The Happy Planet Index measures what really matters – long and happy lives now and the potential for good lives in the future."

Nic Marks, New Economics Foundation fellow and creator of the Happy Planet Index

The Index ranked 151 countries using global data on life expectancy, experienced well-being and ecological footprint.

Each of the three components were given a traffic-light score: good (green), middling (amber) and bad (red) performance.

Top ten countries and UK for comparison

Rank	Countries	Life Expectancy	Well-being	Footprint	HPI Score out of 100
2050 target		87.0	8.0	1.7	89.0
World average		69.9	5.3	2.7	42.5
1st	Costa Rica	79.3	7.3	2.5	64.0
2nd	Vietnam	75.2	5.8	1.4	60.4
3rd	Colombia	73.7	6.4	1.8	59.8
4th	Belize	76.1	6.5	2.1	59.3
5th	El Salvador	72.2	6.7	2.0	58.9
6th	Jamaica	73.1	6.2	1.7	58.5
7th	Panama	76.1	7.3	3.0	57.8
8th	Nicaragua	74.0	5.7	1.6	57.1
9th	Venezuela	74.4	7.5	3.0	56.9
10th	Guatemala	71.2	6.3	1.8	56.9
41st	UK	80.2	7.0	4.7	47.9

HPI score colour key

- All 3 components good
- 2 components good, 1 middling
- 1 component good, 2 middling
- 3 components middling
- Any with 1 component poor
- 2 components poor, or "deep red" footprint

Like most other high income countries, the UK's low overall score is caused by its large ecological footprint – if everyone consumed as much as the UK we would need almost 3 planets to maintain our consumption.

Whilst many high-income countries score low because of their large Ecological Footprints, the lowest income countries in sub-Saharan Africa tend to rank even lower because of low life expectancy and low well-being.

Bottom ten countries

Rank	Countries	Life Expectancy	Well-being	Footprint	HPI Score out of 100	HPI score colour key
2050 target		87.0	8.0	1.7	89.0	All 3 components good
World average		69.9	5.3	2.7	42.5	2 components good, 1 middling
142nd	South Africa	52.8	4.7	2.6	28.2	
143rd	Kuwait	74.6	6.6	9.7	27.1	1 component good, 2 middling
144th	Niger	54.7	4.1	2.6	26.8	
145th	Mongolia	68.5	4.6	5.5	26.8	3 components middling
146th	Bahrain	75.1	4.5	6.6	26.6	
147th	Mali	51.4	3.8	1.9	26.0	Any with 1 component poor
148th	Central African Republic	48.4	3.6	1.4	25.3	
149th	Qatar	78.4	6.6	11.7	25.2	2 components poor, or "deep red" footprint
150th	Chad	49.6	3.7	1.9	24.7	
151st	Botswana	53.2	3.6	2.8	22.6	

Spain (62nd) and Greece (83rd) are now experiencing economic difficulties and huge unemployment – they are within the top ten fallers in happiness levels.

The results show that we are still not living on a happy planet

Source: Happy Planet Index, New Economics Foundation (nef)
www.happyplanetindex.org
www.neweconomics.org

SEE ALSO:
www.completeissues.co.uk

Countries that kill

Only 10% of countries in the world carried out executions in 2011... a drop of more than a third over the last decade

At least **676** people were **executed** worldwide. It is also believed that **thousands** are executed in **China** but the numbers are hidden. Also the full number of executions in Iran is unknown.

People were executed or sentenced to death for a range of offences including:

- **adultery** and **sodomy** in **Iran**;
- **blasphemy** in **Pakistan**;
- **sorcery** in **Saudi Arabia**;
- the **trafficking of human bones** in the **Republic of Congo**; and
- **drug offences** in more than 10 countries.

Methods of execution in 2011 included **beheading, hanging, lethal injection** and **shooting**.

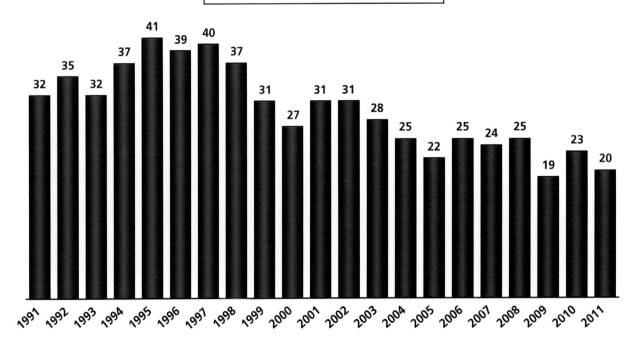

The number of countries carrying out executions 1991-2011

Year	Count
1991	32
1992	35
1993	32
1994	37
1995	41
1996	39
1997	40
1998	37
1999	31
2000	27
2001	31
2002	31
2003	28
2004	25
2005	22
2006	25
2007	24
2008	25
2009	19
2010	23
2011	20

Sub-Saharan Africa
Somalia (10)
South Sudan (5)
Sudan (7+)

The Americas
USA (43)

Asia-Pacific
North Korea (30+)
Bangladesh (5+)
Vietnam (5+)
Taiwan (5)
Afghanistan (2)
China (+)
Malaysia (+)

For the first time in 19 years, there were **no executions** recorded in **Japan**

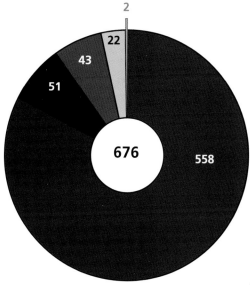

Executions by region, 2011

2
22
43
51
676
558

Europe & Central Asia
Belarus (2)

Middle East
Iran (360+)
Saudi Arabia (82+)
Iraq (68+)
Yemen (41+)
Gaza (3)
United Arab Emirates (1)
Egypt (1+)
Syria (+)

"+" after a number – the true figure is **at least** that shown

"+" without a number – **more than one** execution or death sentence in that country but not possible to obtain any figures – counted as 2 in the global and regional totals

In the **Middle East** there has been a steep rise in recorded executions, **up** almost **50%** on 2010. This was due to four countries – **Iran, Saudi Arabia, Iraq** and **Yemen** – and accounted for **99%** of all recorded executions in the Middle East and North Africa.

Public executions were carried out in **Iran, North Korea, Saudi Arabia** and **Somalia**.

The **United States** was the only country in the Americas to execute prisoners. **34** states retain the death penalty and **13** carried out executions in 2011.

At least **1,923** people were known to have been **sentenced to death** in **63** countries in 2011 and at least **18,750** people were **under sentence of death** worldwide at the end of 2011.

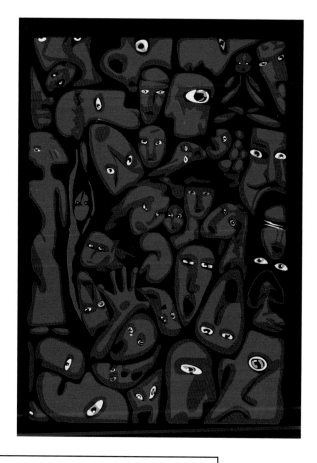

More than two-thirds of the countries in the world have now abolished the death penalty in law or practice.

Source: Amnesty International
www.amnesty.org

SEE ALSO:
www.completeissues.co.uk

Hungry

One in seven people in the world will go to bed hungry tonight

Hunger is the world's number 1 health risk

AIDS, MALARIA AND TB

HUNGER

Hunger = malnutrition.

Malnutrition means lack of some or all the nutrition needed for health.

There are more hungry people in the world than the combined populations of the USA, Canada and the EU.

There are 925 million hungry people in the world – 98% of them live in developing countries

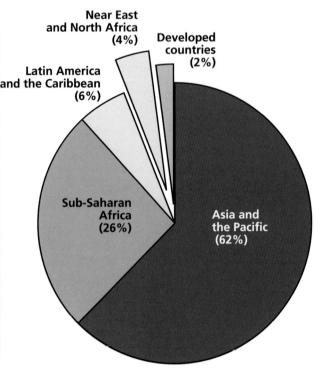

Where the world's hungry people live

Near East and North Africa (4%)

Developed countries (2%)

Latin America and the Caribbean (6%)

Sub-Saharan Africa (26%)

Asia and the Pacific (62%)

Long-term malnutrition causes devastating and irreversible damage. Lack of nutritious food, along with infection and illness, means bodies and brains don't develop properly – this is known as **stunting**.

1 in 4 of the **world's** children are **stunted**. In **developing countries** it is **1 in 3.**

80% of stunted children live in just **20 countries**

At least **170 million children** are affected by **stunting**. If current trends continue, the lives of more than **450 million children** globally will be affected in the next 15 years.

Photo: Hector Conesa / Shutterstock.com

% of children under five who are stunted

Region	%
South Asia	47%
West and Central Africa	40%
Eastern and Southern Africa	39%
Middle East and North Africa	28%
East Asia and Pacific	19%
Latin America and Caribbean	15%

Every hour of every day, 300 children die because of malnutrition

Malnutrition is an underlying cause of the death of **2.6 million children** each year.

Sources: United Nations World Food Programme; A life free from hunger © Save the Children Fund 2012; World Hunger Education Service; Childinfo
www.wfp.org/hunger/stats
www.savethechildren.org.uk
www.worldhunger.org
www.childinfo.org

SEE ALSO:
Going without, p176-177
www.completeissues.co.uk

Going without

The world's poorest families are having to cut back on food

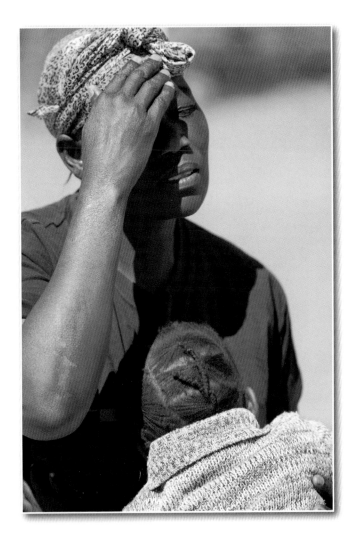

925 million people live in poverty and hunger because of high food prices and the global economic crisis and this number is likely to rise.

Many of the poorest children are living on low cost basic foods such as white rice, maize or cassava. These have very low nutritional value. Yet the world's poorest people already have to spend **between 60% and 80% of their small income on food**. And food prices are rising.

Half the world's malnourished children live in Bangladesh, India, Nigeria, Pakistan and Peru.

A survey of 6,672 adults in these five countries showed the struggle to feed their children.

The people who are most likely to struggle are those who have more than one child, are less educated or have a low income.

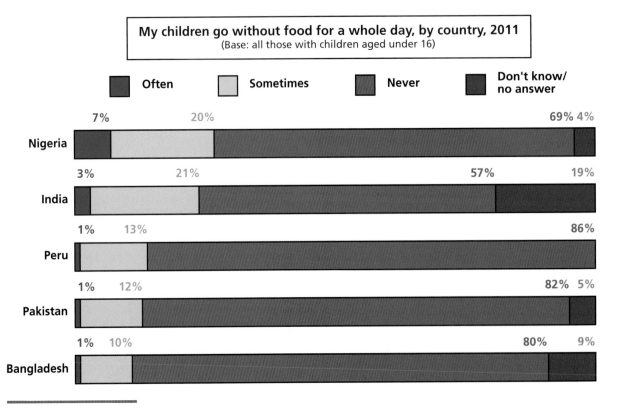

My children go without food for a whole day, by country, 2011
(Base: all those with children aged under 16)

| Often | Sometimes | Never | Don't know/ no answer |

Country	Often	Sometimes	Never	Don't know/no answer
Nigeria	7%	20%	69%	4%
India	3%	21%	57%	19%
Peru	1%	13%	86%	
Pakistan	1%	12%	82%	5%
Bangladesh	1%	10%	80%	9%

30%

of parents in **Nigeria** had allowed their children to skip school to work to help pay for food since the rise in food prices. This is more than any other country.

The majority of parents in Nigeria

58%

also said their children complained about not having enough to eat – **12%** of these said it was **often**.

" ...nearly a quarter of a billion parents in countries already struggling with malnutrition have cut back on food for their families **"**

Justin Forsyth, Chief Executive of Save the Children

Photo: Lucian Coman/Shutterstock

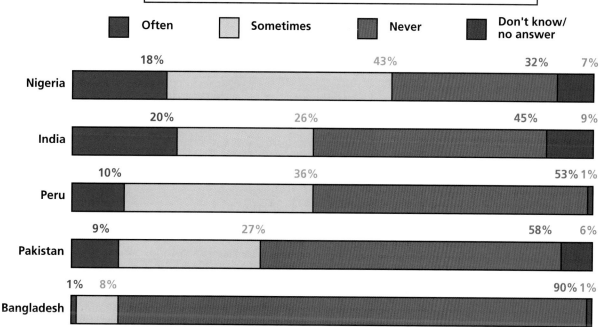

My family eats one staple food such as maize, rice or bread, and nothing else, for at least a week, by country, 2011

- Often
- Sometimes
- Never
- Don't know/ no answer

Country	Often	Sometimes	Never	Don't know/no answer
Nigeria	18%	43%	32%	7%
India	20%	26%	45%	9%
Peru	10%	36%	53%	1%
Pakistan	9%	27%	58%	6%
Bangladesh	1%	8%	90%	1%

"The world has made dramatic progress in reducing child deaths, down from 12 to 7.6 million, but this momentum will stall if we fail to tackle malnutrition"

Justin Forsyth, Chief Executive of Save the Children

*Source: Food and Agriculture Organization,
Globescan Multi-Country Nutrition Poll 2011*
© Save the Children Feb 2012
www.fao.org
www.savethechildren.org.uk

SEE ALSO:
Hungry, p174-175
www.completeissues.co.uk

Born too soon

Every year, 15 million babies are born prematurely – and this number is rising

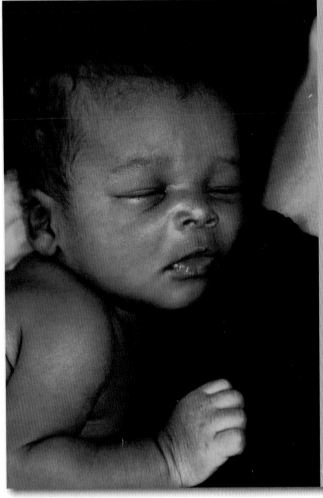

The Facts:

- The full term of a pregnancy is normally 40 weeks from conception to birth. Babies born alive before 37 weeks of pregnancy are called **preterm.**

- Preterm birth is the leading cause of deaths in newborn babies (those in the first four weeks of life).

- Worldwide, **more than 1 in 10** babies are born preterm every year.

- **Over 1 million** children die each year due to the complications of preterm birth.

- The survival chances of the 15 million preterm babies born each year vary dramatically depending on where they are born.

- In low income countries **over 90%** of babies born earlier than 28 weeks die within the first few days of life. In high income countries **fewer than 10%** of such babies die.

South Asia and sub-Saharan Africa...

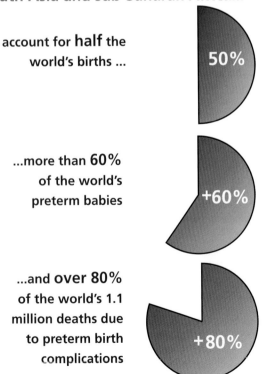

account for **half** the world's births ... **50%**

...more than **60%** of the world's preterm babies **+60%**

...and **over 80%** of the world's 1.1 million deaths due to preterm birth complications **+80%**

"It is very striking to see that preterm births have a similar burden all around the world - but due to different reasons.

In developing countries it is due to things like infections, HIV, malaria and poor nutrition.

In developed countries there are totally different risk factors - an older delivery age, diabetes, obesity and multiple births due to IVF."

Dr Lale Say, World Health Organization

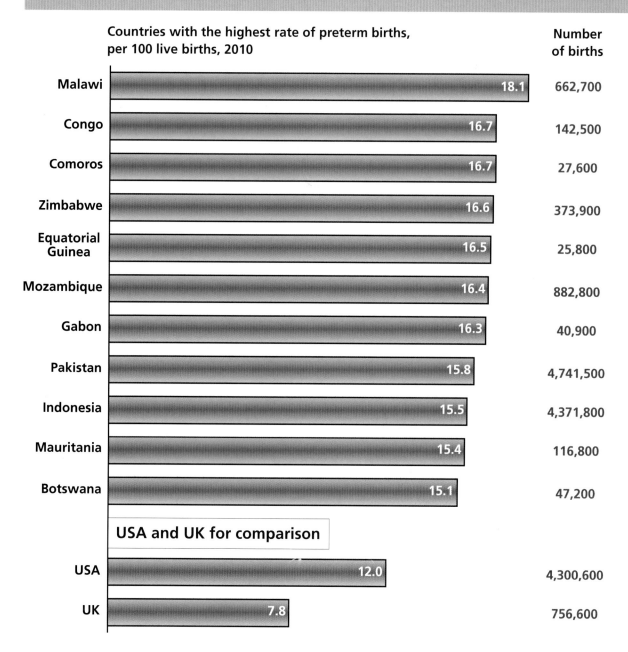

Countries with the highest rate of preterm births, per 100 live births, 2010	Number of births
Malawi — 18.1	662,700
Congo — 16.7	142,500
Comoros — 16.7	27,600
Zimbabwe — 16.6	373,900
Equatorial Guinea — 16.5	25,800
Mozambique — 16.4	882,800
Gabon — 16.3	40,900
Pakistan — 15.8	4,741,500
Indonesia — 15.5	4,371,800
Mauritania — 15.4	116,800
Botswana — 15.1	47,200
USA and UK for comparison	
USA — 12.0	4,300,600
UK — 7.8	756,600

The risk of death due to complications of preterm birth is **at least 12 times higher** for a new born African baby than for a European baby. Yet **more than three quarters** of premature babies could be saved if a few inexpensive treatments were available eg steroid injections given to pregnant women at risk of preterm labour to strengthen the babies' lungs, antiseptic cream for the umbilical cord and antibiotics to treat newborn infections.

Source: World Health Organization –The Global Action Report on Preterm Birth, 2012
www.who.int

SEE ALSO:
www.completeissues.co.uk

Critical contraception

The use of contraceptives is a key factor in fulfilling three of the UN Millennium Development Goals...

 4 Reduce child mortality
 **5** Improve maternal health
 6 Combat HIV/AIDS

Logo ©UNESCO

... and can contribute directly and indirectly towards achieving all eight goals. The other five are: tackle poverty, education, gender equality, environmental sustainability, further development.

In developing countries, there are **867 million** women of reproductive age who do not want a pregnancy within the next two years who need access to contraception. Of these **74%** are using **modern methods** such as the pill.

The remaining **222 million** are using **no method** or **traditional methods** (these are much more likely to fail than modern methods). These women are classed as having an **unmet need**.

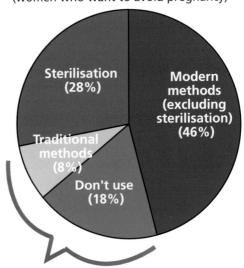

Use of contraception in the developing world
(women who want to avoid pregnancy)

- Sterilisation (28%)
- Modern methods (excluding sterilisation) (46%)
- Traditional methods (8%)
- Don't use (18%)

Unmet need

Women with an **unmet need** made up **26%** of those who wanted to avoid a pregnancy, but they accounted for **79%** of the **80 million** unintended pregnancies...

Use of **modern contraceptives** in the developing world will prevent:

- **218 million** unintended pregnancies which will avoid **55 million** unplanned births;
- **138 million** abortions, **40 million** of them unsafe;
- **25 million** miscarriages; and
- **118,000** maternal deaths.

Source: UNFPA, Adding it up; Costs and Benefits of Contraceptive Services – Guttmacher Institute, June 2012
www.unfpa.org
www.guttmacher.org

SEE ALSO:
www.completeissues.co.uk

Work

Unequal earnings

Your pay level can depend on where you live, how old you are and whether you are male or female

Average full-time gross* weekly earnings, by occupation and gender
£ per week, April 2011

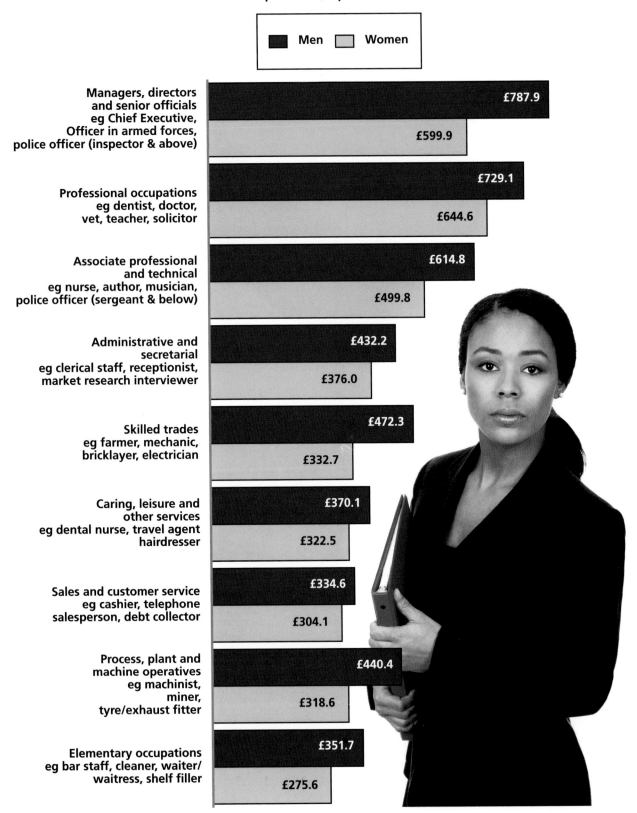

Men ■ **Women** ▢

Managers, directors and senior officials
eg Chief Executive, Officer in armed forces, police officer (inspector & above)
- Men: £787.9
- Women: £599.9

Professional occupations
eg dentist, doctor, vet, teacher, solicitor
- Men: £729.1
- Women: £644.6

Associate professional and technical
eg nurse, author, musician, police officer (sergeant & below)
- Men: £614.8
- Women: £499.8

Administrative and secretarial
eg clerical staff, receptionist, market research interviewer
- Men: £432.2
- Women: £376.0

Skilled trades
eg farmer, mechanic, bricklayer, electrician
- Men: £472.3
- Women: £332.7

Caring, leisure and other services
eg dental nurse, travel agent hairdresser
- Men: £370.1
- Women: £322.5

Sales and customer service
eg cashier, telephone salesperson, debt collector
- Men: £334.6
- Women: £304.1

Process, plant and machine operatives
eg machinist, miner, tyre/exhaust fitter
- Men: £440.4
- Women: £318.6

Elementary occupations
eg bar staff, cleaner, waiter/waitress, shelf filler
- Men: £351.7
- Women: £275.6

*gross = before any deductions for tax, insurance etc.

How old are the highest and lowest earners?

Average full-time gross weekly earnings by age

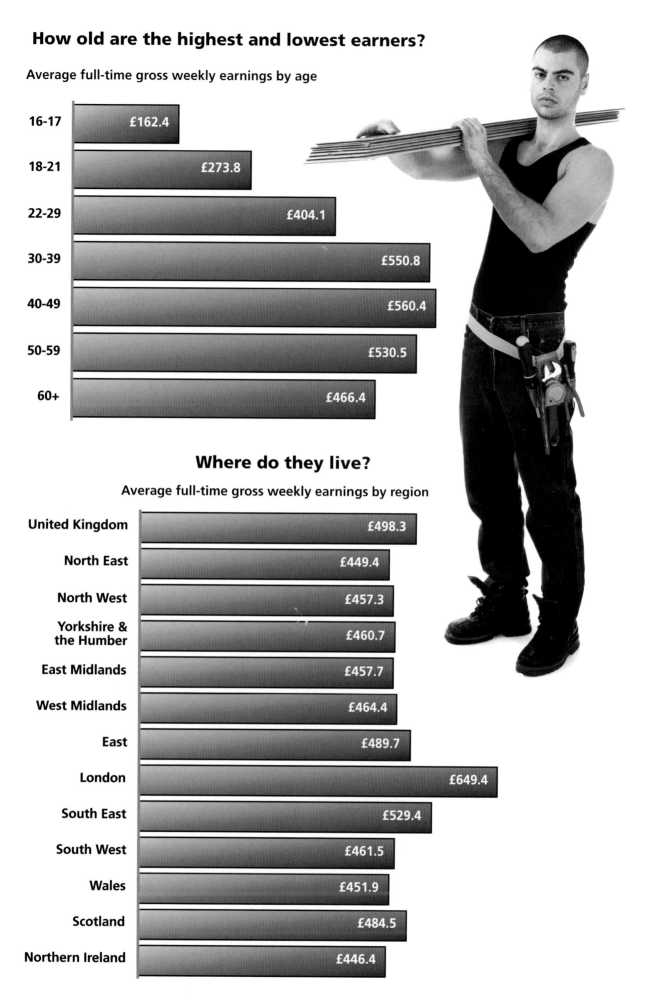

Age	
16-17	£162.4
18-21	£273.8
22-29	£404.1
30-39	£550.8
40-49	£560.4
50-59	£530.5
60+	£466.4

Where do they live?

Average full-time gross weekly earnings by region

United Kingdom	£498.3
North East	£449.4
North West	£457.3
Yorkshire & the Humber	£460.7
East Midlands	£457.7
West Midlands	£464.4
East	£489.7
London	£649.4
South East	£529.4
South West	£461.5
Wales	£451.9
Scotland	£484.5
Northern Ireland	£446.4

Source: Office for National Statistics Annual Survey of Hours and Earnings 2011 © Crown copyright 2012 www.ons.gov.uk

SEE ALSO:
www.completeissues.co.uk

Bare minimum

Almost everyone who works in the UK should get a minimum level of pay

The **National Minimum Wage** (NMW) sets minimum hourly rates that employers must pay their workers.

In 2011 there were **297,000** jobs paid below the NMW held by people aged 16+, equivalent to **1.2%** of all employee jobs in the labour market.

You can be paid more than the NMW but you must not be paid less

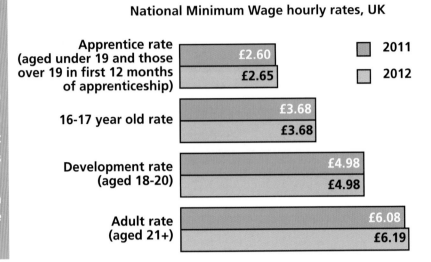

National Minimum Wage hourly rates, UK

■ 2011
□ 2012

Rate	2011	2012
Apprentice rate (aged under 19 and those over 19 in first 12 months of apprenticeship)	£2.60	£2.65
16-17 year old rate	£3.68	£3.68
Development rate (aged 18-20)	£4.98	£4.98
Adult rate (aged 21+)	£6.08	£6.19

How did the UK adult minimum wage rate in 2011 compare to other countries?

France	£7.86
Australia	£7.73
Netherlands	£7.37
Belgium	£6.98
Ireland	£6.86
New Zealand	£6.31
UK	£6.08
Canada	£5.90
US	£5.67
Japan	£4.83
Greece	£4.16
Spain	£3.62
Portugal	£2.87

Source: Low Pay Commission; HM Revenue & Customs; Office for National Statistics © crown copyright 2012
www.lowpay.gov.uk
www.hmrc.gov.uk
www.ons.gov.uk

SEE ALSO:
www.completeissues.co.uk

Pulling a sickie

Why some people miss work when they're not genuinely ill

An online survey of 2,278 people of which 1,337 were in full or part time work.

23% admitted to being **dishonest to their boss** in order to have some time off

11% were in **full health** when they took sick leave

12% said they were **too hungover** to work

19% said they were **too tired to** get up

12% called in sick even though they were **probably well enough** to go to work

39% of those surveyed pulled a sickie because they just **didn't want to go** into work

12% said they **had plans** and didn't want to use up their holiday allowance

A separate online survey of 2,010 UK adults found that:

18% had already taken at least **one day** sick In the first two months of 2012

Those who had taken sick leave had taken an average of **four days** off in the first two months of 2012

Source: Opinium
www.opinium.co.uk

SEE ALSO:
Happy Workers?, p186-187
www.completeissues.co.uk

Happy workers?

Happiness at work comes from a sense of well-being and respect, as well as the actual job

A survey of 13,582 adults 18-65 years old and 1,276 companies in seven European countries: Austria, Belgium, Denmark, France, Germany, the Netherlands and Sweden rated happiness levels on a scale of 1 to 10, where
10 = Very happy and
1 = Very unhappy

Happiness in the workplace

Happiness with actual job

The difference in scores between happiness at work and happiness with their actual job shows that people have found work that suits them, but don't necessarily feel they fit into the company they work for.

Up to **85%** of employees would look for another job if they were unhappy in their organisation, even if they felt happy in their job.

Happiness in life versus happiness at work

People's happiness at work is linked with happiness at home.

In life, the **happiest** people in Europe are people in **Denmark** and **Sweden**.

The next happiest are the **Germans** – but while they are **happy in life**, they are the **least happy at work**.

Austrian workers are **not very happy at work** either.

People in **Belgium** are **happiest at work** on average, followed by the **Danes** and the **Dutch**.

The majority of Europeans are **happy in life** and **happy at work**

Unhappy in life but **happy at work**

Happy in life, but **unhappy at work**

Unhappy both in **life** and **at work**

> "Happy workers get more money, have more opportunities for promotion, deliver more quality, make fewer mistakes, and are more productive and committed"
>
> *Leo Bormans Ambassador of Happiness & Quality of Life*

Reduced absenteeism

Unhappy employees will use any excuse to stay away from work. Long term unhappiness can also result in depression and mental illness.

But happiness at work encourages employees to get the work done. The survey showed that **84%** of happy workers would be more likely to go to work even when they felt a bit ill.

Top ten factors a business can use to influence happiness at work

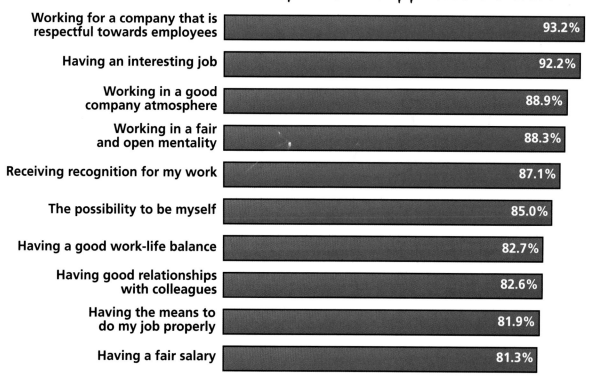

Factor	Percentage
Working for a company that is respectful towards employees	93.2%
Having an interesting job	92.2%
Working in a good company atmosphere	88.9%
Working in a fair and open mentality	88.3%
Receiving recognition for my work	87.1%
The possibility to be myself	85.0%
Having a good work-life balance	82.7%
Having good relationships with colleagues	82.6%
Having the means to do my job properly	81.9%
Having a fair salary	81.3%

Employers grossly overestimated their employees' happiness

Their average happiness estimate for employees was **7.2 out of 10** – quite a difference from the **5.1 out of 10** the employees actually said!

SEE ALSO:
Pulling a sickie, p185

Source: Happiness at work – StepStone
www.stepstone.com

www.completeissues.co.uk

Hit hard

The financial crisis has hit the youth of Europe hard – as shown by employment rates before and after it started

Youth unemployment rates in European Union countries, which are also members of the OECD*

(Percentage of total youth labour force, 15-24 years old)

	December 2007	March 2012
Greece	21.6	51.2
Spain	19.7	51.1
Portugal	19.7	36.1
Italy	21.3	35.9
Slovak Republic	19.4	33.9
Ireland	9.4	30.3
Hungary	19.9	28.4
Poland	18.5	26.7
Estonia	7.3	24.9
Sweden	19.3	22.8
EU average	15.1	22.6
UK	13.6	21.9
France	18.3	21.8
Finland	16.2	19.4
Czech Republic	9.6	19.0
Luxembourg	15.1	17.4
Belgium	17.3	17.1
Slovenia	11.5	16.5
Denmark	7.1	15.1
Netherlands	6.4	9.3
Austria	7.3	8.6
Germany	11.4	7.9

*The Organisation for Economic Co-operation and Development is an international economic organisation of 34 countries committed to democracy and the free-market economy.

Bulgaria, Cyprus, Latvia, Lithuania, Malta and Romania are EU countries but not members of the OECD

Source: OECD via Eurostat, May 2012
www.oecd.org
ec.europa.eu/eurostat

SEE ALSO:
www.completeissues.co.uk

From the other side

Why aren't employers taking on young people?

Employers who had not taken on a young person in the last 12 months gave the main reasons as: **no suitable roles 41%** or were **not recruiting at all, 28%**. However **28%** mentioned a **lack of knowledge** about the job or a **lack of skill** and

22% said they would prefer someone with **more experience**.

Only **12%** of employers were put off by **lack of literacy and numeracy skills** and **10%** felt there were problems with the **attitude** of young people.

What about those who did employ young people?

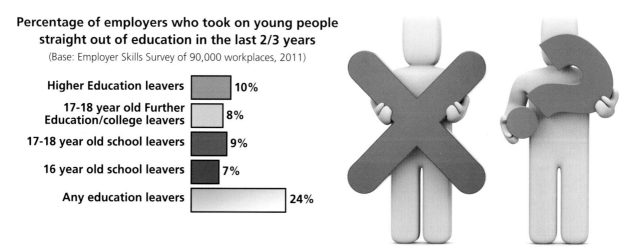

Percentage of employers who took on young people straight out of education in the last 2/3 years
(Base: Employer Skills Survey of 90,000 workplaces, 2011)

Higher Education leavers	10%
17-18 year old Further Education/college leavers	8%
17-18 year old school leavers	9%
16 year old school leavers	7%
Any education leavers	24%

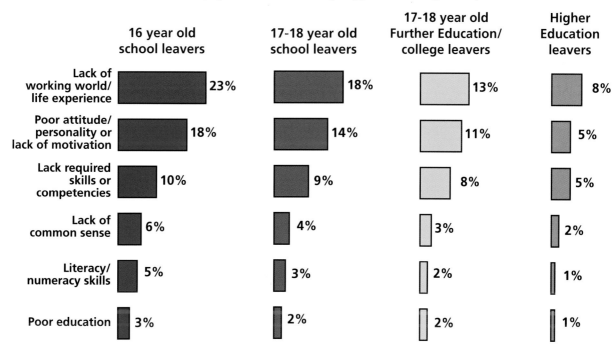

Proportion of recruiters of young people who find them poorly or very poorly prepared, by reason
(Base: all employers who had recruited a young person in each age cohort)

	16 year old school leavers	17-18 year old school leavers	17-18 year old Further Education/college leavers	Higher Education leavers
Lack of working world/life experience	23%	18%	13%	8%
Poor attitude/personality or lack of motivation	18%	14%	11%	5%
Lack required skills or competencies	10%	9%	8%	5%
Lack of common sense	6%	4%	3%	2%
Literacy/numeracy skills	5%	3%	2%	1%
Poor education	3%	2%	2%	1%

The main factor holding young people back is lack of experience.
It seems they cannot gain work without experience and cannot gain experience without work.

Source: The Youth Employment Challenge,
UK Commission for Employment and Skills
www.ukces.org.uk

SEE ALSO:
www.completeissues.co.uk

Fact File 2013 • www.carelpress.com

Work **189**

Effects of unemployment

Large numbers of young people are not in work, education or training, with devastating effects on their emotional wellbeing

Percentage of 16-24 year olds not in education, employment or training (NEET), England 2000 to Quarter 2, 2012

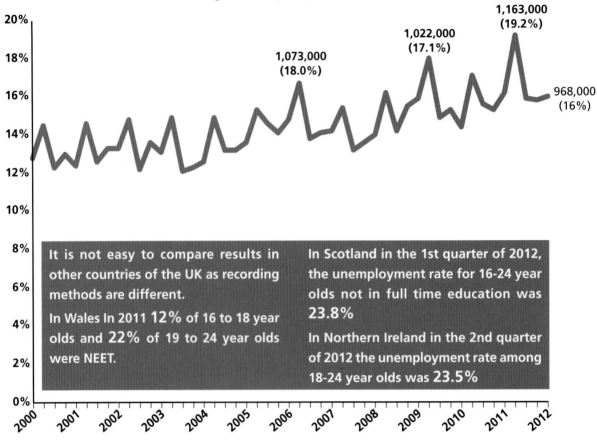

1,073,000 (18.0%)

1,022,000 (17.1%)

1,163,000 (19.2%)

968,000 (16%)

It is not easy to compare results in other countries of the UK as recording methods are different.

In Wales In 2011 **12%** of 16 to 18 year olds and **22%** of 19 to 24 year olds were NEET.

In Scotland in the 1st quarter of 2012, the unemployment rate for 16-24 year olds not in full time education was **23.8%**

In Northern Ireland in the 2nd quarter of 2012 the unemployment rate among 18-24 year olds was **23.5%**

NB: The spikes in the graph mostly occur in the 3rd quarter – July, August and September

The Prince's Trust asked young people about how happy and confident they feel

Not in education, employment or training

In education, employment or training

	Felt happy	Felt confident
Not in education, employment or training	58	62
In education, employment or training	74	75

The responses were converted to numbers out of 100.

A score of **100** would mean **entirely happy or confident** and **zero** would mean **not at all happy or confident**.

Most young people have quite high scores, but there is a significant difference between those who are NEET and the rest.